To Al, at Christmas 1972

from your cousins, Paul and Renée

Nature's Ways

HOW NATURE TAKES CARE
OF ITS OWN

LET US A LITTLE PERMIT NATURE TO

TAKE HER OWN WAYS; SHE BETTER UN-

DERSTANDS HER OWN AFFAIRS THAN WE.

Montaigne

NATURE'S WAYS

HOW NATURE TAKES CARE
OF ITS OWN

By Roy Chapman Andrews

ILLUSTRATED BY ANDRE DURENCEAU
AND OTHERS

CROWN PUBLISHERS, INC. · NEW YORK

PLANNED AND PRODUCED

BY THE

CREATIVE BOOKMAKING GUILD, INC.

UNDER THE DIRECTION OF

GEORGE HORNBY

MANUFACTURED IN THE UNITED STATES

OF AMERICA

PUBLISHED SIMULTANEOUSLY IN CANADA

BY GENERAL PUBLISHING COMPANY LIMITED

The Plan of This Book

THIS is a book on nature and the many strange and wonderful ways in which nature's creatures have equipped themselves for survival. It is a presentation in general and of course, in the compass of this one volume, cannot be encyclopedic. Nevertheless, the information and illustrative material contained herein is organized for ease of reference and maximum usefulness. Following the Table of Contents there is a *Classified* Table of Contents listing the animals according to their most notable ways of protection—protective coloration, mimicry, speed, etc. Furthermore, the Index lists each creature discussed in the book by all its popular names as well as by its scientific name.

Acknowledgments

MANY individuals and organizations were helpful in the preparation of this book, and the debt of the author and the publishers is hereby acknowledged to The American Museum of Natural History, New York Zoological Society, and the National Audubon Society.

The publishers are especially thankful to the Travelers Insurance Companies for that organization's courtesy in permitting the use of its color plates.

To the many who contributed their time and effort in the gathering of picture material and in helping to make this book thorough and authoritative, the author and publishers hereby extend full gratitude.

Table of Contents

Note: All the color reproductions in this book are from paintings by André Durenceau, except as otherwise noted in this Table of Contents.

Classified Table of Contents

WARNING SIGNALS

DEFENSIVE ARMOR AND OFFENSIVE DEVICES

SPECIALIZATION

ADAPTATION

FOOD-STORING AND FORAGING DEVICES

SYMBIOSIS

INTRODUCTION

During my entire life, I have had a consuming interest in animals. Many different kinds have been my pets, and for forty years, as a naturalist, I studied and collected mammals, birds, fish, reptiles, and lizards. Exploring expeditions for the American Museum of Natural History took me into the remote corners of almost every continent; the study was continued at home in Connecticut and Arizona, or wherever I chanced to be.

To me, one of the most fascinating aspects of nature is the way it equipped every creature, be it of high or low degree, to withstand enemies and to obtain the necessities of life. Some animals had to change their entire physiology or anatomy to enable them to meet competition and to survive; more often less drastic adaptations in skin, color, or habits made the difference between life and death of a species in the struggle for existence.

I remember how dramatically the nature of concealing colorations was brought home to me when I was hunting a man-eating tiger in Fukien Province, South China, in 1916. For three hours I had sat motionless behind a screen of bushes at the entrance to the lair. Two goats, a mother and her nursing kid, tied fifteen feet away, bleated incessantly. It was a devilish place, a deep cut in the mountain choked with thorny vines and sword grass. Suddenly the mother goat gave a terrified bleat, and tugged frantically at her rope, staring across the ravine. Just within the edge of the grass beside the palm tree, I saw a great yellow and black striped head. I rubbed my eyes. It wasn't there a moment before; it had taken shape and substance, ghostlike, out of nothing. It was a tigress—a man-eater—the one I had come to kill. She seemed to suspect danger, seeing the goats in that unusual place with no Chinese near them. She crouched beside the tree like an enormous tabby cat, sometimes stretching one foot forward as if about to move, but each time drawing it back again.

At last the tigress rose and circled to reach a tiny path. I could follow her progress by the moving grass. She had to cross a small bare space—it was only about twenty feet, but apparently she didn't like being in the open. She flattened like a snake, her chin and throat touching the ground, and slithered along with no body motion that I could see, except the quivering of her shoulders and hips. Yet she went very fast. Once in cover again, she disappeared like a wraith even though the grass was thin. Only when a bush swayed slightly did I realize that I was looking directly at her. The outline of her body gradually took shape, but the yellow and black stripes merged so perfectly with the light and shade of the sword grass that she was well-nigh invisible.

For another ten minutes she crouched motionless, staring at the goats. Then she made three flying leaps up the terrace. The last one brought her face to face with me, not fifteen feet away. Utterly surprised, she stood there snarling, ears laid back, her green eyes blazing. My nerves tightened. Sighting low on her breast, I squeezed the trigger. The heavy rifle slammed against my shoulder like a kicking mule. The tigress threw up her head, reared back and slid slowly down the terrace. For five minutes I watched the body but there was not the slightest movement. The man-eater was dead.

CONCEALING AND PROTECTIVE COLORATION

Lighting my pipe, I sat down on the edge of the rice dyke, thinking of what had happened. How the great beast had materialized, seemingly out of nothing; how startlingly visible the black and yellow stripes made her in the open, but how she faded into the grass when she gained the cover. What superb camouflage! Had her body been all yellow, or any solid color, I would have seen her instantly. Her life was spent in the thickest jungle and she knew that there she was invisible. "Concealing coloration," not "protective," in her case, for she had few natural enemies. Only a wild buffalo or an elephant would tangle with a tiger, and never willingly, but she had to eat. Her food was the game of the jungle. Nature made it possible for her to live by giving her the advantage of bodily concealment to pit against the keen eyesight and smell and hearing of the beasts she stalked. She hunted on the ground where her stripes matched the coarse, upstanding grass.

But what about the black-spotted leopards and jaguars? Both are essentially tree cats. Lying along the big lower branches, they drop on their game from above; less often they stalk it on the ground. Their spots blend perfectly with the dappled light and shadows of the leaves.

Strangely enough, man was slow to apply the principles of camouflage to his own uses. Not until a talented artist, Abbott Thayer, brought it to universal attention forty years ago was it adopted extensively in war. Many of us can remember the ships, fantastically striped and dotted, lying in our

The Leopards' spots blend with the dappled light and shadows

harbors during the first World War. Breaking up the solid colors so that the outline of a vessel at a distance was confused even on the flat surface of the sea: that was the idea. The tiger stripes and the leopard spots on a ship! This was carried to excess, at first. Later, camouflage became an important factor for both army and navy. Our soldiers in World War II, fighting in the tropical jungles of New Guinea and the Pacific Islands, used helmets and clothes, dotted and striped with contrasting colors. A long way from the British red coats and the Union blue less than a hundred years ago.

Abbott Thayer enunciated another important principle of concealment that nature had developed: counter shading. It is the simple natural law that many animals have the back and upper parts dark, where they receive most light, and shade gradually into white, or a lighter color, on the lower sides and belly which receive least light. This graduation tends to make the animal less visible than if the color were uniform above and below. Thayer, like most enthusiasts, carried his theory much too far, insisting that concealing coloration of one kind or another applied to *all* individuals of the animal kingdom, whether of high or low degree.

That, of course, is nonsense, and it subjected him to verbal attacks from many naturalists, but the basic element of his discovery, counter shading, is an easily demonstrated fact. Even though the late Colonel Theodore Roosevelt was one of his severest critics, he wrote a long paper entitled *Revealing and Concealing Coloration in Birds and Mammals* on which, it so happened, I worked with him. The Colonel painted life-size, cardboard silhouettes of our common Virginia deer in its winter coat, with and without counter shading. In the woods at Oyster Bay, we placed them among bare branches, leafless bushes, and in the open against the deer's natural forest background. Then we walked backward away from them. It was amazing how quickly the counter-shaded "deer" disappeared from sight, while those painted a solid color remained visible for many yards.

Geography has an important bearing on concealing coloration. As a general rule, animals of the arctic and northern regions are white or lightly colored. The polar bear, living among the ice floes, is always white, enabling him more easily to stalk the seals which are his principle food. So, also, is the arctic wolf, the Peary caribou, the arctic fox, the Dall sheep of the snow-covered mountain slopes, and the arctic hare. Further south, the grouse-like ptarmigan goes through an amazing change to keep itself always protectively colored. During the winter the bird is pure-white and invisible in the snow unless it moves, but the spring moult coincides with the changing season and provides it, for a time, with a patchwork plumage of white and brown that makes it resemble a snow-dotted hummock or rock. If the season is late, the moult is late. Its brown summer plumage harmonizes perfectly with the grass of its nesting site.

Similarly, nature has protected the varying hare, giving it a white winter pelage, mixed brown and white in the spring, and counter-shaded brown during the summer. Weasels are the only carnivores which change from the brown of summer to a white winter coat. Their small size, and the need for activity to obtain food in the snowy northern regions where they would be peculiarly susceptible to danger from birds of prey and the larger predatory animals, make the protection of white winter coats necessary.

The Polar Bear, living among the ice floes, is always white

In the deserts, most ground birds, mammals, reptiles, and insects are pre-vailingly brown or sand-colored, either for protection or concealment in their hunting operations. On the other hand, the tropics, with an abundance of heavy vegetation and vivid flowers, tends to encourage brilliant colors.

When it comes to recounting instances of individual protective coloration, I am confronted with an embarrassment of riches. Most of the lower forms of animal life—particularly those that have sedentary habits and "stay put" in a constricted area, like worms, insects and various invertebrates—depend upon resemblance to their surroundings and immobility to render them in-conspicuous both for their own protection and for securing the food upon which their lives depend. There are thousands of examples of which I will quote only a few of the more typical. Among the birds, my mind turns to the woodcock as an excellent example of what nature has done to care for her own, both in protective coloration and adaptation. The woodcock, "tim-berdoodle" to every sportsman, is a lover of alder swamps and moist birch groves. Its plumage so perfectly matches the brown leaves and grass that it is invisible even to the keenest eyes. Dozens of times my setter dog has pointed a woodcock nestling on the ground within a few inches of his nose, but still I could not see it. It was literally a part of its surroundings. Since the woodcock drives its three-inch bill deep into the ground, searching for earthworms with the highly sensitive tip, and never sees what it eats, the bird's eyes have migrated up and back toward the top of the head, so that when it is engaged in feeding it can watch for enemies from either side and behind. The ruffed grouse is quite as protectively colored as the woodcock, and adds supreme cleverness in escaping enemies as an additional safety factor. Night hawks and whippoorwills reinforce their protective resemblance by always resting lengthwise on a limb. Only by chance can one distinguish a night hawk from a piece of bark.

Certainly camouflage is not the only one of nature's ways employed by man for his own uses. Rather, it is amazing to see how many of man's "ingenious" devices were long ago developed naturally by one creature or another—bifocals, blackouts, periscopes—ad infinitum. Perhaps a further study of nature's solutions will suggest to man additional "ingenious" devices needed for his special problems.

MIMICRY

Mimicry is closely akin to protective coloration, but differs in that the true mimic resembles a conspicuous "model" feared or disliked by its enemies. Mimicry is infrequent in mammals, birds, and fishes, but poisonous snakes are often models for harmless species. The puff adder, *Heterodon contortrix,* is a conscious mimic of rattlers. *Elaps,* the dangerous and warningly colored snake, is a model for several nonpoisonous species, and the South African egg-eating reptile, *Dasypeltes scaber,* mimics the Cape adder. *Oxyletis,* of Honduras, which feeds largely upon chameleons, resembles the vegetation among which it lives. It "freezes" into position on a branch, and is virtually indistinguishable from the surrounding twigs.

The Sargasso Sea, discovered by Christopher Columbus in the South Atlantic, is a vast area of seaweed which slowly, almost imperceptibly, rotates and supports a great quantity of strange sea organisms that depend for their safety upon mimicking the vegetation among which they live. Weedlike fishes, weedlike crabs, and weedlike slugs, some of which can change color to imitate their background, form a fantastic world of their own in this great floating mass.

Even plants mimic others. For instance, the stinging nettle is the model for the dead nettle with which it is commonly associated. But insects are the supreme mimics. Bees and wasps are models for several inoffensive flies, and ants for many insects of diverse kinds. The butterfly *Kallima* has developed a color pattern on the underside of the wings which is a replica of a dead

PUZZLE: FIND THE INSECTS

You can hardly distinguish these two *Bazillus rossii*
from the twigs they mimic

leaf. The green body of the Ceylonese walking leaf is shaped and veined exactly like a leaf, and the larva of the moth *Amphidasis* mimics a rose twig. Some insects even mimic reptiles. Snakes are models for caterpillars, and experiments have demonstrated that such mimicry is effective in terrifying monkeys, birds, and lizards, which are their mortal enemies.

IMMOBILITY

Although nature has provided protection for many of her children in coloration, she has given all of them an immeasurably greater asset in the inherited instinct of immobility. Remaining absolutely motionless, "freezing," is the most potent factor in safeguarding an animal's life. Even a highly colored bird, reptile, mammal, or insect will often escape notice if it remains motionless in its natural habitat. The most dramatic example that I remember of the value of immobility to a conspicuous animal occurred when I was hunting black gibbons in the wilderness of Yunnan, near the Tibetan frontier. Our tents were pitched on a ridge. The sides fell away in steep slopes clad with spreading trees, their branches interlaced to form a solid roof of green above the soft moss-carpet underneath. We had hardly made camp when the forest resounded with the "hu-wa, hu-wa, hu-wa" of a herd of gibbons on the march. Grabbing a rifle, I dashed down the slope while the

American Museum of Natural History

The Gibbon, master of immobility

wild, ringing cries came nearer and nearer. At last I saw the apes catapulting from branch to branch, traveling through the forest faster than a man could run. Suddenly they were right above my head, their black bodies strikingly visible among the green leaves. The tree swarmed with monkeys; there must have been thirty of them. Just as I stepped from behind a bush, a great ape saw me and hung suspended by one arm for a moment, his round head thrust forward, staring intently. Then, with a startled, high-pitched "hu-wa," he swung upward and disappeared in a splash of leaves. One moment the tree was alive with swinging black bodies; the next, it was as quiet as the grave. The apes had vanished as though into thin air.

I knew they were all close above my head, but I could not see a sign of life. I sat down a few yards away and waited, motionless. After half an hour, a slight stirring in the leaves caught my eyes. A black form rose cautiously from atop a branch not ten feet away and crept forward. I fired quickly. At the roar of my rifle, the tree seemed to burst into violent activity as the black apes swung in twenty-foot leaps through the forest down the hillside.

Almost every creature knows, instinctively, that no matter how well its color blends with the surroundings, absolute immobility is its best protection. The slightest movement makes for betrayal. I once watched a rabbit in brown grass for half an hour. It was six feet away, and during that time I could not see the tremor of a muscle even though a fly alighted on its nose and crawled upward across one half-shut eye. The spotted fawn of our Virginia deer lies in deathlike immobility where its mother has placed it after birth. In a dense tropical forest, even such huge beasts as elephants and buffalo are difficult to see in the mass of gloom, the occasional lights, and amid protecting tree trunks, vines, and ground vegetation so long as they remain immobile. Brilliantly colored birds, like scarlet tanagers, cardinals, and orioles, know that in the foliage among the upper branches of a tree they have reasonable protection if they do not move.

SPEED

To many species of animals, the survival of the fittest has meant the survival of the fastest. An insect, the deer bot fly, *Cephenomyia pratti*, is the speed champion of the world. A rate of four hundred yards per second, or eight hundred and eighteen miles an hour, has been chalked up for him—*him*, because, for obvious reasons, the female does not fly so fast. That speed has been estimated by the best scientific observations. Still, I would feel more comfortable about Cephenomyia's reputation if it were possible to subject it to tests in a wind tunnel. That being out of the question, we must accept the word of Dr. Charles H. T. Townsend, a scientist who has devoted many years to the study of insects, and this one in particular.

[23]

The Jumping Rat, *Jerboa,* is notable for both speed
and adaptation. See page 173

In an article in the *Journal of the New York Entomological Society* (Vol.
XXXV), Dr. Townsend writes: "Regarding the speed of Cephenomyia, the
idea of a fly overtaking a bullet is a painful mental pill to swallow, as a
friend has quaintly written me, yet these flies can probably do that to an
old-fashioned musket ball. They could probably have kept up with the shells
that the German Big Bertha shot into Paris during the World War. The
males are faster than the females, since they must overtake the latter for
coition. Then the males habitually fly at higher altitudes than the gravid
females, and thus encounter less friction which enables them to attain
greater speeds. . . . On the other hand, on 12,000-foot summits in New
Mexico, I have seen pass me at an incredible velocity what were quite certainly the males of Cephenomyia. I could barely distinguish that something
had passed—only a brownish blur in the air of about the right size for these
flies and without sense of form."

Dr. Townsend says in a letter: "The time was checked repeatedly with
the shutter of a camera. The data are practically accurate and as close as
ever will be possible to measure." If one could drive an airplane at the
speed of Cephenomyia for seventeen hours continuously, one could go
around the world in a daylight day. The "Saber Jet," the fastest plane man
has yet developed, in tests reached only six hundred and seventy miles per
hour.

Although Cephenomyia flies at high altitudes where air resistance is reduced, in the lowlands of New Jersey there lives a considerably larger fly

[24]

The Addra Gazelle, one of the swiftest of animals

which can take off from a twig with such velocity that it is utterly impossible to see where it has gone.

As a matter of fact, it is not surprising that insects can claim the speed championship of the world. They have been flying longest. Birds have been on the earth only for a paltry one hundred and thirty-five million years, whereas a heritage of several hundred million years in nature's trial-and-error flying school lies behind the insects. The birds, however, have not done so badly. It is difficult to measure their speed accurately, but probably the chimney swift is one of the fastest of them. It is estimated that when feeding it flies at a rate of seventy miles per hour. Personally, I believe that is much too conservative an estimate. A great bearded vulture was once pursued by an airplane and went into a nose dive at a velocity of one hundred ten miles per hour by the plane's speed indicator. However, it is hardly fair to call this flying speed. The golden eagle has been clocked at one hundred twenty miles per hour and the duck hawk (hunting) at one hundred sixty-five to one hundred eighty miles. It seems unlikely that this extreme speed could be maintained by the bird unassisted by a tail wind.

Fish, and other creatures of the water, have attained a wonderful beauty of movement, but the density of water presents a handicap that keeps them far "out of the running" in the matter of sheer speed. The flying fish, however, has developed an effective way to elude its enemies by launching itself into the air. The fish attains the high velocity necessary for a take-off after it has emerged but before it has lifted its tail quite out of the water. The fish "taxies" for a take-off just as a seaplane does, and after gathering speed for from five to twenty yards it can take off in any direction, even down-wind. The speed it attains at the end of the "taxi" is probably about thirty-five miles an hour, according to the observations of Dr. Carl L. Hubbs, of the Scripps Oceanographical Institute, and others. The flying fish does not beat the air with "wings," like a bird, but merely supports itself in the air. In this respect, and in the form of the body, the flying fish more closely resembles an airplane than does any other flying creature.

In the Gobi Desert we made with our cars the first accurate tests of an antelope's speed. We found that the desert gazelle could reach sixty miles per hour. How long it could maintain that rate we did not discover. The photographer of my expedition, James Shackleford, and I chased one fine buck for ten miles; the race ended when we got a puncture, but he didn't stop. Of course, the great speed of the initial dash is to save them from wolves, their most important enemy.

The Gobi wolves, by the way, cannot do better than thirty-six miles an hour and can kill an antelope only by concealing themselves in a ravine, or behind a bush, and by waiting until the animals are very close. The Mongolian wild ass has a maximum speed of forty miles per hour for at least a furlong, or perhaps half a mile. Not all are able to reach that speed, but none is slower than thirty-five miles an hour. They, too, can outdistance their enemy, the wolves, on the first rush. The hunting leopard, or cheetah, is supposed to be the fastest animal for a short distance. It is built to overtake its prey in a flashing dash and can do one hundred yards at a speed of seventy miles per hour. But it could not run a mile anywhere near as fast.

Dr. William K. Gregory, of the American Museum of Natural History, has revealed an interesting relationship between anatomy and speed. In the fast animals, like the horse and the antelope, he points out that the lower leg bones are longer in proportion to the upper, and that these animals achieve their great speed by a rapid snap-kick stride. The action of a man wielding a golf stick illustrates the principle. Flexibility of spine also enters into the case. The greyhound, for instance, is enabled to take a much longer stride than he could with a rigid backbone. But the important thing seems to be the length of the distal elements, shin and foot, and the proximal elements, the thigh bones.

Knowing that speed is its greatest protection from enemies, the Gobi gazelles seek a wide, flat plain when giving birth to their young. There, a mother can watch and entice enemies away from her baby just as a bird simulates a broken wing and flutters off from her nest when an intruder appears. The gazelle fawns are able to run within a few minutes of birth. Their brown, counter-shaded bodies remain absolutely motionless, with necks stretched out and ears down. I have often tried to catch a newly born fawn by throwing my coat over it, but at the last instant, when it realized it had been discovered, it leaped to its feet and wobbled away. After a day or two, a baby gazelle can outrun a horse.

SIGHT

Nature has endowed some animals, and many birds, with incredibly keen eyesight both for protection and to enable them to obtain their food. Vultures, wild geese, and ducks have eyes as sensitive as radar. Often, on the Gobi desert, after killing and then skinning an animal, I would leave the carcass. With ten-power binoculars I would scan the heavens in every direction and then sit down some distance away to time the arrival of the black vultures, one of the largest birds in the world. Usually, in not more than fifteen or twenty minutes, I could pick out tiny specks in the sky with the field glasses. Wheeling in wide circles, the great birds would drop lower and lower, finally to land upon the carcass. Doubtless they had been watching the skinning operation from far beyond the range of human sight. For many years naturalists believed that vultures depended as much upon smell to find food as upon their eyes, but this has been effectively disproved.

Wild geese and ducks have "telescope eyes" and are remarkably clever in avoiding danger. Their hearing is good, too, but eyesight is their principal safety factor. A white swan is one of the most conspicuous objects in nature, and the birds depend almost entirely upon their eyes, keeping well away from suspicious cover, and nesting on the flat tundra where an enemy is visible for miles.

SMELL

Some animals, particularly wild sheep, deer, and bears, have developed the sense of smell to an astonishing degree. In the Altai Mountains of Mongolia, where I hunted giant bighorn sheep, I was provided with an excellent example. A herd of sheep, containing some magnificent rams, usually fed on a steep slope in the early morning. When the sun was high, they retired to a narrow ridge connecting two peaks, with deep ravines on either side, to sleep away the midday hours in plain sight. Always an old ewe acted as a sentinel. For an hour or more, after the sheep were lying down, she would stand on a rocky spire above the saddle, gazing in every direction over the plains and mountain slopes. At last, satisfied that it was safe, she would settle herself with the rest of the herd. Then my Mongol hunter and I would begin the stalk, being sure that the wind was blowing from them to us. But never could we approach near enough for a shot. Always the herd was up and off. At last we realized that the reason they selected this particular ridge day after day, and attempted no concealment, was because the air eddied in a peculiar way about the saddle and brought odors to their noses no matter from what direction the wind was blowing. On that saddle the sheep were as safe from wolves, their only natural enemy, as from man.

The black bear relies on an extremely delicate sense of smell and a fine sense of hearing, but has poor eyesight. The great Alaskan brown bears, the largest carnivores in the world, have such keen noses that the taint left by a man's recent tracks, or the faintest odor on the breeze, starts them off at full speed. All the deer family depend much more upon their noses for protection than upon either eyes or ears. From my own experience, I have come to the conclusion that a deer's sight is comparatively poor, although its hearing is far better than a man's and its sense of smell exceedingly acute. If wind is blowing toward a deer, elk, or moose, one might as well not attempt a stalk. Wolves and dogs have wonderful noses and, of course, in some domestic species the sense of smell has been improved by selective breeding. But the champion "smeller" of the world is a moth. The moth can scent a female, during the breeding season, more than two miles away.

WARNING SIGNALS

The warning signal is another of nature's protective methods. The pronghorn antelope trusts largely to eyesight and speed, but also possesses a rump patch of long, pure-white hairs. When the animal is alarmed, this expands into a chrysanthemum-shaped disc, and by rapid opening and shutting sends warning flashes like a heliograph. On the plains it is visible for miles. I have seen a herd of peacefully grazing antelope suddenly throw up their heads and dash away in headlong flight. They had seen warning flashes from

The Pronghorn Antelope showing the white rump patch which by
rapid opening and shutting sends warning flashes like a heliograph

the rear ends of other pronghorns far away and knew that somewhere
danger lurked.

The antelope jack rabbit of Mexico is a member of the group of jack rabbits in which the white of the underparts extends well up on the sides of
the body. This assists in producing one of the most extraordinary examples
of directive coloring known among mammals. The late Dr. E. W. Nelson,
former Chief of the U. S. Biological Survey, writes: "As I rode slowly along,
a big jack rabbit hopped deliberately from its form in the grass a few yards
away, and by contraction of a special set of muscles along the back drew
the dark-colored dorsal area forward and together so that it formed only a
narrow band on the middle of the back, with a corresponding extension of
the white area on the rump and sides until, as the animal moved diagonally
away, it looked almost entirely white.

"At a distance of fifty or sixty yards it came to a stop and expanded and
contracted the dark dorsal area, thus producing a 'flashing' effect with the
changing area of white on the sides and rump. This solved the riddle of the

[29]

mirror-like flashes I had often seen as jack rabbits on the tableland dashed away in the brilliant sunshine."

It is probable that the light-colored rump patches or tails of wild sheep, deer, rabbits, and smaller animals are warning signals to others of their kind. Perhaps, also, they act as recognition marks enabling members of the herd to keep together, but to my mind that is not the primary reason for their development.

The hoary, or whistling, marmot of our high northwestern mountains emits a warning whistle that is one of the most piercing sounds in nature. It can be heard easily for a mile and when conditions are right, double that distance. Every marmot within reach of the sound scuttles to its hole. When the danger is past the sentry-marmot sounds a lower note that appears to be the "all clear" signal. Then, all over the mountainside, gray heads pop out of the ground and the marmot world resumes its business.

The beaver can produce an effective alarm signal. When the animal is frightened, or disturbed, it strikes the surface of the water a resounding slap with its broad flat tail. Every beaver within hearing distance, and that is a long way on a still night, disappears as if by magic. I have often heard it on a beaver pond when my canoe came in sight of the first animal.

Warning colors are associated with some quality or weapon, such as un-palatability, poison fangs, or an evil odor. Skunks carry a "beware" sign in the conspicuous, flaunting tail which waves over their backs. They are slow-moving beasts, never in a hurry or willing to be hurried, for they know they can throw out a stench cloud that no animal can tolerate. It also informs other skunks that danger is imminent. Rattlesnakes warn their enemies with a whirring buzz of the tail. Cobras rear up, sway slowly back and forth, spread the hood and show the strange "spectacle" marking. Many other creatures use signals, either for their own protection or to warn others of their kind to seek safety in their individual ways.

ARMOR

Animals developed armor and spines to preserve themselves from harm millions of years before man came upon this earth. In the far, dim days, before the Age of Dinosaurs, the most popular of all styles in apparel for fishes was a stiff suit of bony scales, movable only along the scales' beveled edges. Then, with the arrival of the huge, newly evolved Pleisosaurs, and other fish-swallowing, bone-crushing monsters in the Age of Reptiles, the former advantages of protective armor were practically nil. Fishes of the Mesozoic seas faced a changing tempo, and nature did something about it. The speed-up movement arrived. Speed, not armament, was necessary.

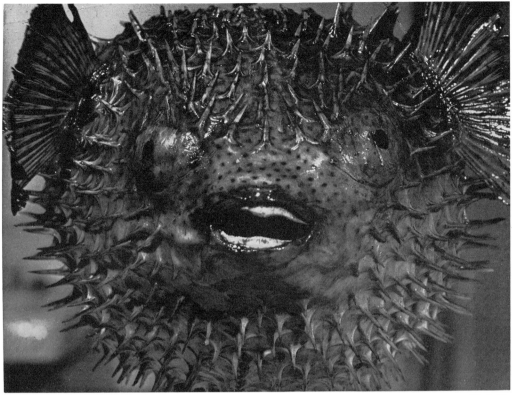

The Porcupine Fish

Nearly all modern fishes have long since discarded the ancient suits of bony armor, but the trunk fishes of tropical American waters have readopted the old-fashioned, prehistoric style of armor suiting, just as man has reverted to certain types of medieval armor in present-day warfare; witness the helmets, breast plates and bullet-proof vests. The scales of the trunk fish's body constitute a solid series of hard, hexagonal plates firmly joined together to form a single inflexible bony case. A tortoise in its shell can move its head in and out and twist it, if it wishes, but the only independent movement of the head that a trunk fish can execute is to ogle its eyes and to pucker its lips. Nevertheless, it gets along, in this modern world of ferocious marauders like barracudas and morays, and does extremely well.

The porcupine fish is another that has armored itself in a different way. The scales are modified and make a globular series of sharply pointed spines. These jagged needles form an effective coat of mail and oppose the enemy from all points of the compass. The South American catfish, on the other hand, is literally sandwiched in between two solid plates of bone. The unfishlike sea horses, that swim so slowly and gracefully through the water by imperceptible movements of their semitransparent fins, are encased in a series of bony rings. The trigger fishes of the tropics have many small, hard, steel-like tubercles in their skin. They are tough-skinned, indeed, but their pugnacious relatives, the file fishes, are even tougher.

Turtles and tortoises are effectively armored by their enclosing shells, and we find a somewhat similar protection among mammals in the armadillo. The upper parts of the body, even the ears, are covered with sculptured horny plates. Porcupines have an effective type of armor in the needle-sharp quills that project from the body in every direction, and the little hedgehog of Europe and Asia is a veritable pincushion. By curling into a ball with its nose tucked between its hind legs, it becomes impervious to attack.

SPECIALIZATION

To my mind, the way nature has provided for the life and comfort of many of her children by adapting them to the peculiar conditions under which they live is more wonderful than any of the other methods we have been discussing. Water is an absolute necessity to most creatures, yet many desert animals never have to drink. Kangaroo rats, pocket mice, prairie dogs, gazelles, wild asses, and dozens of other species, both large and small, pass their whole lives without touching a drop of water. The liquid necessary for their bodily needs is obtained through chemical action in their digestive tracts whereby some of the starchy parts of their food are changed into water. I kept a gazelle as a pet for half a year in the Gobi, and not once did it drink. In Southern California, pocket mice were kept captive for months in a box and fed solely upon thoroughly dried seeds without showing the slightest sign of discomfort.

Hardly less remarkable is the way animals can put themselves into cold storage to weather a period when their food is unobtainable. In the northern parts of the world, bears, marmots, prairie dogs, ground squirrels, jumping mice, and others pass a great part of the winter in hibernation. They go to sleep in the fall and do not apear until spring. While hibernating, these animals have extremely slow, slight heart action, and their blood temperature falls far below normal. Their bodily functions appear to be practically suspended and the animals may be said to be in cold storage. How easy it would be for us to solve the high cost of living could we hibernate during part of the year!

Some mammals, such as pocket gophers and moles, found competition above ground so acute that they took to the unoccupied territory below the surface, where they live as miners and tunnel from place to place in search of food. Whales and seals went into the water for the same reason.

Others, perhaps because of their small size and defenselessness against birds and beasts of prey, have put their faith in darkness. Hundreds of species of small mammals, and untold millions of individuals, appear only at night and live such obscure and hidden lives that they are almost unknown to humans. With the beginning of darkness a countless multitude of insects and small beasts comes forth, swarming out from nests and burrows in the earth, from crevices among the rocks, from hollow trees, and from under logs. In number and variety of forms, they far exceed anything seen by day. The air is filled with bats, velvet-winged owls, night hawks and whippoorwills; on the ground are rabbits, rats, mice, lemmings, pocket mice, shrews, and even moles. But the abundance of night-life brings forth the prowling powers of darkness in the form of weasels, skunks, martens, and other carnivores. They in turn are subject to the predatory law of might, and at times are hunted by the larger flesh-eaters, such as wolves, foxes, fishers, and wild cats. Every one, whether it lives by night or day, has its mortal enemy.

ADAPTATION

Modifications of parts and organs fit certain animals for a specialized life. Some alterations are profound, others less so. Whales are, perhaps, the most completely modified of all mammals, for their physiology and anatomy have been completely changed to adapt them to an aquatic existence. Seals are only partly transformed, since they live both in the water and out of it. Flying squirrels have developed a connecting membrane between the front and hind limbs so they may glide through the air. Bats have gone still further, and the skin uniting the lengthened limbs and long finger bones forms broad wings enabling them to fly as well as birds and catch their insect food in the air. Nature has also given them a radar set enabling them to avoid obstacles by echo. Gophers, pocket mice, chipmunks, and squirrels have cheek pouches in which they carry food home to their storerooms; hares have exceedingly long legs for running, and weasels have long slender bodies allowing them to follow their prey into burrows and among crevices in the rocks. Kangaroos and other marsupials have remarkable pouches in which to carry their young. The long tails of kangaroo rats and jumping mice serve as balances for their bodies during long leaps. The tails of muskrat and beaver are useful as rudders, and the naked tail of the opossum can coil about branches and permit the animal to hang suspended by it alone. Some lizards have tails that break off easily but continue to move, and certain crabs can shed their claws.

I have mentioned comparatively few creatures which have survived as

A fish with wings: the flying fish, *Cypselurus heterurus*

the result of unusual characteristics, habits, or adaptations. All over the world, in almost every spot on the globe, in its waters or in the air, are animals suited to live in that particular environment under the conditions prevailing there, and, perhaps, nowhere else. How did they manage to fit themselves for survival? The answer, of course, is in the constant struggle for existence. Every creature has two great requirements: food and protection from its enemies. The competition is never-ending, and each animal must vie not only with other species but with others of its own kind. In the course of time (and by that I mean many millions of years), the ineffectives are weeded out and die, but those that develop the ability in one way or another to cope with their environment are the ones that live.

The tigers with concealing coloration were able to get more food than those that did not have it, and their progeny were more numerous than the less effectively colored tiger's. Animals that learned how to "freeze" survived where animals that had not developed that ability were killed off. The fastest deer bot fly reached the female first, and the result of that union served to perpetuate speediness in the species. Everyone knows that the principle of thoroughbred racing is in breeding a fast horse with a fast mare. If a fast horse is mated with a slow mare, the chances of getting fast foals are much reduced.

Then there is another side to the matter—when, for some reason or another, a habitat becomes insupportable. Some animals will be able to leave it, find a more congenial place, and adjust themselves to the changed conditions. In time, they will develop new habits in the new environment and new methods of protection or anatomical variations. These adaptations also include the loss of faculties, organs or members, through disuse and eventual atrophy, such as the hind legs of whales which now exist only as rudimentary bones, buried deep in the body. Probably natural selection has more to do with these adjustments than any other law of nature, but how far natural selection suffices for the production of species remains to be seen. Few can doubt that, if it is not the whole cause, it is a very important factor, and that it must play a great part in the sorting out of varieties into those which are transitory and those which are permanent. Whether or not the actual acquired characters are transmitted from one generation to another is a debatable point, but the *ability* to respond to the environment certainly is transmitted.

The ape-man who first got the idea of standing up didn't find it easy to do so, but his children found it a little easier, especially because he probably trained them to stand erect almost from birth. In any case, they would imitate him—as would other men who perceived the greater success in living that standing erect permitted.

Walter E. Higham, F.R.P.S., F.I.B.P.

The Gannet alighting with full brakes on. This bird is a "dive-bomber," notable for its speedy vertical dives from heights of 100 feet or more. Conversely, it can stop short as shown here.

I have presented in this introduction some of the more dramatic examples of how animals meet the tremendous competition of mere existence. Most of the creatures shown in the book are strange and curious, but included also are some familiar animals which, because we are used to them, do not seem remarkable at all. Yet every one is notable in some feature, has achieved distinction in preparing itself for life's struggles. Anyone who will take the trouble to observe what is about him can find countless others. But now, enough of this talk; let's look at the exhibits.

Nature's Ways

HOW NATURE TAKES CARE
OF ITS OWN

The Fish With the Built-in Bifocals

IN the quiet rivers and estuaries of the Caribbean lives an unusual fish named *Anableps dowei*.

He is only about five to seven inches long; he prefers to feed on tidbits which float on the surface of the water. Therefore it is necessary for him to see in the air as well as in the water.

The way *Anableps* has met what seems like an insoluble ocular problem is really marvelous. Each of his eyes has two pupils, one above the other. The upper pupils, which are out of water when the fish is at the surface feeding, admit light through the short dimension of the lens. The lower pupils admit light through the long dimension of the lens. As *Anableps* goes along, he can see trouble through any dimension above or below, through air or through water.

Humans who must wear bifocals or spectacles would feel themselves fortunate if, like *Anableps*, the two parts of their glasses were part of themselves and hence unlosable and unbreakable.

Not only can he see above and below while he is at the surface, but his air eyes have need of moisture, which in most animals is provided by eyelids and tear glands. Since *Anableps* has neither, every few minutes he ducks his head under water to wet the upper eyes.

The Gila Monster Stores Food in His Tail

YES, the Gila monster is definitely poisonous in spite of what you may have heard to the contrary. Don't pick it up and annoy it, or you may be sorry. It will endure a good deal of irritation, but if it clamps down on your hand, it hangs on like a bulldog with its grooved teeth while poison oozes out between them and the lower lip from glands in the jaw. The idea that the Gila monster is not poisonous originated because it and its close relative, the beaded lizard of Mexico, are the only living venomous lizards.

Among superstitious people, the notion is prevalent that the Gila monster has no anus. The poison, they say, comes from accumulated waste that must be voided through the mouth.

No one would wish to pick up a Gila monster except for scientific examination or out of curiosity, for it is about the most repulsive-looking reptile in the world. The monster is usually about a foot long and covered with a beadlike skin resembling an old fashioned beaded-bag. Its coloration is a sickly yellow or salmon, blotched with black.

The Gila monster has developed a curious solution to the problem of survival through times of food shortage. The thick, ungainly tail acts as a food reservoir, storing up nourishment for the reptile, to be used during times when forage is scarce. When food is plentiful, the tail becomes thick and swollen. When food is scarce the tail is thin and attenuated.

The Inventor of the "Blackout" and Jet Propulsion

IN war time, when a naval vessel wants to escape a pursuing fleet, it often lays down a smoke screen and moves away behind the black curtain. That is exactly what the octopus does. Only it was utilizing this method of defense long before man came upon the earth.

If a wolffish or an eel finds an octopus, the eight-armed creature squirts into the face of its enemy brown or black fluid, which looks like India ink, from a bag concealed within the body. Behind this smoke screen, the octopus can wriggle away and hide itself in a crevice of the rock. Moreover, the octopus (or devilfish) has still another method of concealment. In its skin are various pigment cells, which can, by contracting or enlarging, produce a wonderful series of color changes. These cells are of many hues—orange, yellow, blue-green, or brown—and have muscular walls which enable them to contract until almost invisible and then expand to many times their former size. The different color cells can expand alone or in combination with the other colors, and enable the animal to produce flashes of rainbow hues over its whole surface. As a devilfish crawls about on the sea bottom, it may change its color instantly from deep chocolate through dull red and brown to gray.

As it encounters sand and rock, the skin is thrown into lumps and ridges

From a painting by Grohe

so that under any conditions the body may be practically invisible.

The octopus utilized jet propulsion long before it was discovered by man. A stream of water from a spacious cavity within the body is directed into a tube or funnel, and drives the animal backward as escaping gases drive a rocket. He can go backward as fast as an ordinary fish can swim, but crawls forward only by means of his flexible, snaky arms and suckers.

The two-spotted octopus (*Polypus bimaculatus*) is the common shore devil-fish of Southern California. But another species has a wide distribution along the coasts of China and Japan as well as along our own shores from Alaska to San Diego.

His Armor Is Made of Sponge

THE sponge crab (*Dromidia antillensis*) has solved in a very unusual way the problem of meeting the hazards of the tropic ocean bottom.

Before he ventures forth, he sees to it that he is provided with a covering of sponge. He cuts this protective coat of armor to fit his oval back exactly, and he makes sure that it fits so snugly that it is difficult to remove. As he grows larger, he provides himself with new coverings of sponge, each one of which he fits to his back, very much as a woman tries on a new bonnet.

Thus covered with his coat of sponge, he merely pulls in his limbs, when danger approaches, and presents his enemies with nothing but a tough and unappetizing surface of sponge.

Nature's Air Raid Wardens

THE whistler, or hoary marmot *(Marmota caligata)*, lives on the upper slopes of the western mountains, from central Idaho to the Yukon River.

He is a big marmot, weighing twenty to twenty-five pounds, related to our common woodchuck. He is a lover of the sun and likes to sprawl on a rock, exposing every part of his body to the sun's rays.

The whistler is a gregarious soul and cannot abide a solitary existence, so he always lives in colonies. He has only two important enemies — the grizzly bear and the golden eagle. These big birds are a constant danger every time the whistler goes into the open to feed. To guard against these feathered marauders, the marmot has devised an air-raid protection system somewhat like man's. He frequently digs shallow shelter holes along the pathways from his burrow to the feeding grounds, and these shelters come in handy when an eagle is sighted.

If one of the marmots sees an eagle or a bear, like an air-raid spotter he immediately gives a piercing whistle. It is his version of an air-raid siren and warns his fellows to take shelter. There can be little doubt that this is the shrillest, farthest-reaching sound made by any mammal. It is easily heard a mile away and under favorable circumstances twice as far.

Once the watchman has given the warning, he goes under ground. When the danger is past, the sentry utters a low, quite different whistle, which appears to be the "all clear" signal. Then gray heads pop up all over the mountainside, and the marmot world resumes its business.

The whistler requires sunlight, and when the outer world is bleak and too cold for comfort, all his vital functions are suspended. The sleeper neither grows nor ages. He has retired to hibernation, the deep deathlike sleep with which nature provides some of her children during periods of food scarcity.

The Rattler's Thermostat

EVEN if a rattlesnake can't see you, don't think he doesn't know you are there. He is a member of the clan of "pit vipers," along with the eastern moccasins and copperheads. A small pit located in the head between the nostril and the eye is responsible for the name of the group.

For a long time no one knew the function of the pit, but a few years ago, Dr. G. K. Noble, of the American Museum of Natural History, discovered that it is a sense organ to detect heat and cold. His experiments were most convincing. He plugged the nostrils of a rattlesnake with cotton soaked in collodion and put adhesive tape over the eyes. Then he swung a warm electric light bulb in front of the reptile's head. The snake would strike unerringly at the bulb even though it could neither see nor smell it. If one of the pits were plugged, the rattler would not strike at the bulb on that side of the head, but would hit it if the warm globe were held on the side where the pit was open. When both pits were sealed, the snake made no attempt to strike.

The buzzing tail is a warning signal to its enemies to keep off, for it does not wish to defend itself unless it is necessary. It is commonly supposed that the age of the snake can be told by the number of rattles, but this is not true. It may produce several rattles in a year, or, while traveling through a rock crevice, scrape off some of the buzzing devices.

In the early spring, rattlesnakes are out in the open during the sunny hours, either crawling around or basking on the rocks. But when summer comes, they seek shelter during the heat of the day and lie in the shade of bushes, or bury themselves in sand with only the flat, spade-shaped head protruding. Soon after sunset they become night rovers.

The hollow fangs act as hypodermic needles and the poison drains out through the tubelike points. When not in use they are folded back against the roof of the mouth. More fatalities are attributed to this species than to any other reptile in the United States.

H. *Armstrong Roberts*

The Bird That Uses Insect Police

HANGING from the great ceiba trees in Central America are strange, sacklike objects about six feet long. Often there are fifty or more on a single branch, swaying in the wind. They are the colony nests of the cacique, or tropical oriole.

The eggs in these nests are looked upon as choice food by many of the cacique's enemies. In addition to the ocelots or forest cats, there are giant lizards and raccoonlike animals which are expert nest-raiders. And, being adept at tree climbing, they can easily reach the eggs even at a great height.

If it were not for the ingenious way in which the caciques provide themselves with a municipal police force, their chances of survival would be poor indeed. To secure this unusual protection, the caciques build their colony on the same branch that holds a large nest of tropical wasps. Although these insects do not seem to be annoyed by the activities of the birds, they are aroused to fury if any intruder tries to push past them. And no animal, however fearless, would twice risk their vicious attack.

As the cacique always makes sure that his police guard is between the nesting colony and the tree trunk, his home is safe. Only if the wasp nest should be destroyed or abandoned would this protection fail him. But then his loss would be complete.

He Can See What's Behind Him

THE tarsier is a monkeylike little beast with a round head, closely set in its shoulders, a froglike face, naked ears, and the most enormous eyes of any mammal in proportion to its size. He is one of the multitude of creatures that choose darkness as protection from enemies. The tarsier (*Tarsius carbonarius*) belongs to a distinct family that lives in the Philippine Islands.

During the day the tarsier is sleepy, dull, and seems to be almost blind, but when the black jungle night closes in on the bamboo thicket where he lives, the pupils of his eyes dilate and he moves about quickly and noiselessly to find his food. His night life might be a continuous nightmare of attacks by owls and other preying enemies were it not for his ability to see in the dark better than any of them.

Without moving his tiny body, the tarsier can turn that head of his, with its great round eyes, so that he can look directly to the rear—almost instantly. And if what he sees alarms him, he can jump six or seven times his length to another bamboo perch and safety. The "eyes have it" and he does very well for himself in a hostile world.

A Knight in Armor

THE armadillos are as completely clothed in armor as was any knight of the Middle Ages. Every inch of the upper part of the animal is covered with beautifully sculptured horny plates. These plates appear even on the ears where they are very small and delicate. Armadillos lack teeth in the front of both upper and lower jaws, and are members of the toothless animal group which includes the anteaters. The foods which they eat are licked up by the sticky surface of their extensile tongues.

As its appearance indicates, the armadillo is a stupid animal living a life of restricted motion. Its hearing and eyesight are poor, and the armor gives it an almost immobile body. These characteristics, combined with a small head hung loosely on a short neck, make it resemble a little pig. It jogs along in its trails from one feeding place to another with the same stiff little trotting gait and a self-centered air. When alarmed, the armadillo immediately runs to the shelter of its burrow, but if caught by a dog or a natural foe, it coils up in a ball.

Armadillo burrows sometimes accommodate strange neighbors. It is reliably reported that one in Texas was found to be occupied by the owner in his den at one end, by a big rattlesnake, and also by a half-grown rabbit, each in a side chamber of its own.

The young, numbering from four to eight, have their eyes open at birth; at that time the armor is as soft and flexible as fine leather. The hardening of the skin is progressive, continuing until the animal completes its growth. As soon as the young are able to travel, they trot along with the old one during her foraging trips.

In the remote past, many species of armadillos, some of gigantic size, roamed the plains of South America, and a number of small species still exist there. These animals are peculiar to America and are most abundant on the southern continent.

New York Zoological Society

He Rolls Himself Into a Ball

THE hedgehog's way of taking care of himself seems to work very nicely for him. His body—about nine inches long, the size of a large rat—is covered with sharp spines. That might seem enough protection but in addition the hedgehog has a special muscle that enables him to curl himself up into a ball when danger threatens. Then he looks like nothing so much as a giant chestnut burr.

There are no hedgehogs in America, though there are a number of species inhabiting Europe, Asia and Africa. The common species is *Erinaceus Europaeus.* Of course, the porcupine will be recognized as the American animal nearest resembling *Erinaceus.*

The Wild Turkey Takes No Chances

THE name "turkey" for this bird has a curious history. Originally the term was applied to the guinea fowl which was brought to Europe by way of Turkey. In the sixteenth century, the new imported bird from America was confused with the African guinea fowl, so that both were known as turkeys. From this, the American bird retains the name.

At the time of the discovery of the New World, turkeys were abundant through much of the vast area between eastern Mexico and New England. Because of their numbers and excellent meat, they were a regular source of food to the Indians and at once became important to the early colonists.

Even though they are so large, a wild turkey is one of the most difficult birds to shoot. Nature gave them marvelous hearing and eyesight, and persecution has rendered them extremely cautious.

If a hunter plans to shoot from a blind, he must build it in stages long before the hunting season starts, so that the turkeys have a chance to become accustomed to it. Even then, if so much as a fallen branch in the immediate vicinity of the blind is disturbed, the keen-eyed, careful turkey will give the place a wide berth.

The nest is a hollow scratched in the ground under cover of a log, thick brush, or other shelter. The hen turkey lines it with grass or a few leaves, and lays from eight to fifteen cream-colored eggs spotted with reddish-brown and lilac. She covers the eggs carefully with leaves and grass when she goes off to feed. Woodsmen say that she almost always flies away, in order that no tracks may betray the site to a fox or a wild cat.

Hundreds of turkeys are killed each year in Pennsylvania, and the birds are still common in many areas in the South. Four varieties of wild turkeys are recognized, ranging from Pennsylvania to Colorado and Mexico.

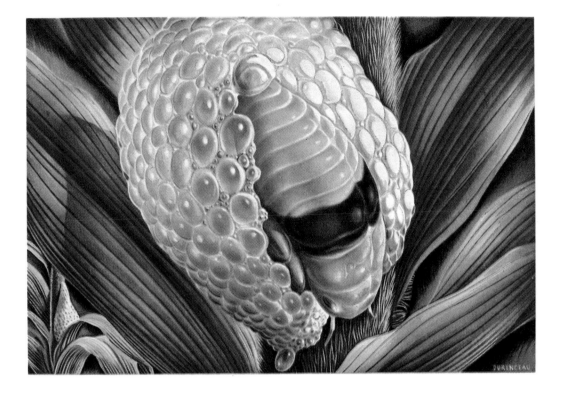

He Makes a Fortress Out of Bubbles

THE cercopid, or froghopper, begins life as an inconspicuous, soft-bodied bug, less than a quarter of an inch long. He is found on plant stems and blades of grass all over America.

There are many insect enemies that are eager to make a meal of him. And he can't run away from danger until the time comes for him to grow wings and jumping legs.

But the froghopper is an ingenious little bug. He builds a fortress. And this fortress is unlike any other found in the insect world.

Soon after birth, he starts secreting a liquid. This he beats into tiny bubbles with his tail until it forms a white froth which gradually covers him.

When the bubble fortress is finished, the froghopper is snugly hidden beneath what looks like a bit of beaten egg white. Perhaps you, yourself, have seen the tiny masses of froth, sometimes called "cuckoo spit," in the fields and woods near your home.

The fluid which forms the bubbles is of a resistant, sticky mixture. In addition to concealing him, it prevents most of the froghopper's enemies from breaking through and seizing him.

The Bear That Lives on Ants

THE grotesque ant bear looks like something out of a nightmare. The long, pointed snout, stiltlike fore legs, rounded shoulders, and tremendous, bushy tail resemble no other beast on earth and mark a high spot in specialization. The ant bears live on the low, swampy savannas along the banks of rivers and in the humid forests of Central and South America wherever they can find termites, their favorite food.

Confronted with an ant hill, the creature digs an opening in the side with its strong, curved front claws. As the termites rush out, the ant bear extends its long tongue, coated with glutinous saliva like fly paper, and sweeps it back and forth among the insects.

The ant bear is a slow moving beast and can easily be overtaken, but it is by no means defenseless. The saberlike front claws can inflict nasty wounds. But, like most animals, it wishes only to be left alone to pursue its inoffensive life among the termites.

It has an effective way of concealing itself during sleep, when it curls its four-foot body into a tight ball wrapped in its enormous, grayish-brown tail and looks like a heap of dried grass.

L. W. Brownell

A Turret Is His Stronghold

IF you see a round hole in the Arizona desert about the diameter of a five-cent piece surrounded by a turret of tiny pebbles, bits of grass or other debris, probably it is the "castle" of a wolf spider. Dig down about eighteen inches and there you will find the grayish-yellow proprietor at home.

During feeding hours he sits on his turret watching for his prey. If an insect ventures within sight, he pursues it like a wolf, brings it to his castle and devours it at his leisure.

Should he be frightened or disturbed all he has to do is to drop down the shaft into the safety of his dwelling.

The Circle Defense

NATURE has not attempted to help the musk ox to survive by giving it concealing coloration, for its dark body against the snow is startlingly conspicuous. Except for man, however, wolves are the only enemies of these cattlelike animals.

They almost always travel in groups of twenty or more. When brought to bay, the herd forms a circle about the calves and with their heads out present a formidable front of sharp horns. As long as the circle remains unbroken, such defense is extremely effective against even a pack of wolves.

Although the animals are heavy-bodied and seem to be clumsy, they can get over the ground with amazing speed. Their eyesight is not good, but their sense of smell is highly developed and the slightest taint of wolf-odor on the wind will send them off like a stampede of buffalo.

The long, coarse outer hair forms a protective raincoat, covering thick, soft under-fur which keeps the animal warm in the coldest blizzard.

Fossil remains prove that the musk ox lived in northern Europe and Asia during the Ice Age, but they have long been confined to Arctic America.

His Beak is Both Scoop Net and Stew Pot

THE white pelican has a large skinny bag which hangs from the lower part of the bill. When distended, this holds several quarts of water and the bird uses it as a dip net to scoop up small fish. It was formerly thought that this pouch served to convey live fish to the little pelicans at home, but it is doubtful whether a pelican could fly at all with so heavy a burden on his neck, which would necessarily throw it out of balance.

One might wonder how such a huge-billed bird could feed helpless chicks just out of the egg. It is done with apparent ease. The old bird regurgitates a fishy soup from the front end of her pouch, and the baby pelican pitches right in and helps himself out of this family dish. As the young birds grow older and larger, they keep reaching further into the big pouch of the parent. The whole neck and head disappear down the mother's capacious maw while it hunts for its dinner in the internal regions.

The American white pelican was formerly found in the east as well as the west, but a bird so conspicuous in size and color has many enemies and can exist only by breeding on some remote island. The largest colonies of white pelicans are found on Klamath Lake and one or two other northwest reservations.

Engineer and Builder

MOST of the rodent family are notable for their weak mental powers, but the beaver is a striking exception to the rule. Its extraordinary intelligence, industry, and skill have long excited admiration.

Beavers live almost entirely on twigs and bark. They will sometimes cut down trees nearly thirty inches in diameter, felling them so skillfully that they fall in the middle of a pond, thus assuring an abundance of food at their very door.

They are proficient in building dams of sticks, mud, and small stones across streams in order to back up water and make ponds where food-trees are plentiful. On the border of these ponds, a conical lodge is constructed of sticks and mud several feet high and eight or ten feet across at the base.

The entrance is usually under water, and a passageway leads to an interior chamber large enough to accommodate the pair and their young. From the ponds, the animals sometimes dig narrow canals one hundred feet long back through the flats among the trees. Thus they can transport by water the sticks and branches needed for food and for the houses and dams. The entire operation is carried out with near-human "engineering" skill.

The mud used by beavers in building dams and houses is scooped up and carried—the front feet being used like hands, the flat tail serving as a rudder and to strike the surface of the water a resounding slap as a danger signal.

When America was first colonized, beavers existed in great numbers from coast to coast in every locality where trees and bushes bordered streams and lakes. They have now been exterminated from most of their range in the eastern United States, but they still occur in diminished numbers in other parts of the country.

The Fish That Convoys Its Young

THE bullhead or horned pout has a well-worked-out method of protecting its fry. When the young fish venture out from their home in some secluded cove, both parents accompany them.

One parent, by swimming around the fry in a small circle, keeps them herded into a compact group about the size of a derby hat, while the other parent swims around them in a much larger circle. At regular intervals, the father and mother fish meet for a moment, exactly as though they were reporting to each other, and change jobs. The inner guard also crosses and criss-crosses through the school.

By this method the bullhead convoys its brood through the dangers of the water, with a minimum of casualties from pickerel, water snakes, and other submarine threats.

Nature's Radar Expert

DON'T worry, ladies, a bat won't get into your hair even though it is flying about the room. Its natural radar set enables it to avoid obstacles by the returning echo of its squeaks and chirps. It would hate being in your hair as much as you would dislike having it there. Some bats have voices so extraordinarily high in pitch that they are beyond the range of human ears, and can only be detected on the sensitive filament of a sound track.

Bats rival birds in their power of flight and are among the most extraordinary adaptations in nature. The skin uniting their lengthened front and hind limbs and finger bones form broad wings which give them marvelous control in darting and turning. No birds, except possibly the chimney swifts, can equal them in their extraordinary gyrations as they feed upon insects.

One of the most unusual characters of the brown bat is the number of young it bears, three or four being the average. When the young are very small, they are carried clinging to the body of their mother in her flights, and she continues to take them from place to place in this manner until their combined weight exceeds her own.

Bats, in spite of their small size, are ferocious fighters. They will bare their teeth, bite viciously, and behave like veritable little fiends.

The brown bat rarely, or never, seeks shelter in small crevices but hangs on leaves or bushes in the full light of the sun. This unusual tolerance of light in a member of the bat tribe is shown another way; it begins to hunt for insects earlier than other species in its range. These bats are often found over ponds and streams, dipping into the water for a momentary drink while they catch their meal of insects.

The Little Haymakers

HIGH up in the mountains on slide rock, near the timber line, from the Urals of Russia through Asia and western North America, there lives a timid, but resourceful, animal called the pika, or little chief hare (*Ochotona princeps*).

He is about the size and shape of a guinea pig with a short, blunt head, short legs, practically no tail, and a long coat of fur; a combination of mouse and rabbit characters.

Owing to his dull-gray or brownish color, the pika blends with the background of slide rock so perfectly that when sitting immobile on a stone, he is extremely difficult to see. But he is ever on the alert. At the first appearance of an enemy, he gives a sharp alarm note, then the whole colony disappears into the shelter of their rocky fortresses.

The pika has many enemies, but the danger which threatens him most is hunger. He lives on grass and other plants. During the summer he can find all he wants to eat; but in winter the slopes are covered by deep snow for many months. Unlike many animals who live in severe climates, the pika does not hibernate. He needs food the year around, so he plans for the winter. Toward the end of summer, he becomes a serious harvester. All day he scampers back and forth from his rockpile home to the weed patches on surrounding slopes. He nips off the stems of short grasses, bundles them together crosswise in his mouth, and runs back to add them to his haystacks.

He spreads them out to dry in the sun like a good farmer, and then packs them away in his "barn," a crevice in the rocks where weather cannot harm the hay. Each barn holds from a peck to a large armful of grass. One stack in the mountains of New Mexico contained thirty-four kinds of plants including many kinds of flowers. When snow comes, because of his foresight, he need only travel from his warm, snug burrow to the barn to find food in plenty. Instinct has made him a happy winter resident.

The Tree That Wears a Petticoat

IN the heart of Africa, there grows a tree known as the silk-cotton tree (*Ceiba pentandra*).

Instead of having a simple, cylindrical trunk, like a maple tree or an oak, the silk-cotton tree has a bole that flares out in folds like a gigantic petticoat.

These folds often begin as high as thirty or forty feet above the ground and form a skirt whose hem line could enclose a small house.

This wooden petticoat serves a very useful purpose. Tornadoes are common in this region. The tree's roots are shallow. And were it not for these tremendous, skirtlike braces, the tree might easily be uprooted.

Where Unity Was Fatal

THERE is no such thing as inexhaustible supply in nature. Witness what has happened to the buffalo and the passenger pigeon! Uncountable millions were here during the colonization of America, but now the passenger pigeon is extinct. The last wild bird of which there is certain record was killed in April, 1904. The end of the species came when the only surviving bird of a flock, long in captivity, died in the zoological gardens in Ohio at 1 P.M., Central Standard Time, on September 1, 1914.

The decimation of these remarkable North American birds has often been attributed to some storm or other natural catastrophe. But it is almost certainly the result of ruthless slaughter by the white man of a bird that had very gregarious habits and no means of defense.

In 1740 Kalm wrote of a flock of pigeons that he had observed in flight in Pennsylvania that was three to four miles long and a mile in breadth. Alexander Wilson told of columns of birds eight to ten miles in length, and the flocks continued for more than an hour in steady procession. He wrote also of a nesting colony in Kentucky that covered an area a mile wide and one hundred thirty miles long. It was not unusual to see a hundred nests in a tree, and the heavy-bodied birds often crowded in groves until large limbs were broken by their weight.

One account says that nine hundred ninety-nine thousand dozen pigeons were shipped in three years from western Michigan to New York City. Another tells of three carloads a day, each containing one hundred fifty barrels of pigeons, shipped from one town for forty days.

L. W. Brownell

Your "Horned Toad" Is a Lizard

SOME horned lizards of the group to which the horned "toad" belongs can eject blood from their eyes for a distance of several feet! With the exception of one type found in Australia, there are no other lizards like them in the world. Our Arizona "horny toad," which children love as pets, isn't a toad at all, of course. He is a true lizard; a flattened, heavy-bodied, short-tailed, spiny, little reptile about four inches long and as gentle and inoffensive as any animal could be.

One can hardly see him on the ground for he is so perfectly desert-colored that he looks like a little mound of brown earth. If he is frightened, he will 'shimmy' from side to side, prying deeper and deeper into the sand until he has disappeared. His tiny nostrils close up tight as he makes his burrow just like a seal's when it swims under water.

Why the Robin Hops — Then Stops

WHEN you see a robin on the lawn stop suddenly, cock its head to one side, and look at you with a bright brown eye, it is not trying to be coy. The bird is listening to the soft stirring of an earthworm under the grass. In a moment you will see it reach into a minute hole and pull out a long, glistening worm. Nature has given it supersensitive hearing, for the satisfaction of its stomach depends upon its ears.

The robin is the best-known and most popular of all wild birds, and its arrival in spring is hailed with joy. Its song at dawn is the first note of the day to millions of human ears. But over vast areas of the Southland, robins are only winter residents, and they neither probe the lawns for worms nor sing in the gardens. There, they frequent open pine woods and feed on half-dried berries hanging in clusters from the trees.

The robin is a good homemaker. It builds a workmanlike nest; a thick bowl of mud held together with blades of grass, reinforced with leaves and weed-stalks, and lined with soft grass. In shaping the mud shell, the mother bird uses her breast, turning around and around. The eggs are so striking and beautiful that they have given their name to a color, "robin's egg blue."

It must be admitted that robins eat a good deal of fruit—cherries, strawberries, etc.—but they also destroy countless noxious insects, and do far more good than harm. To most of us, the robin is our outstanding bird citizen and a cherished friend.

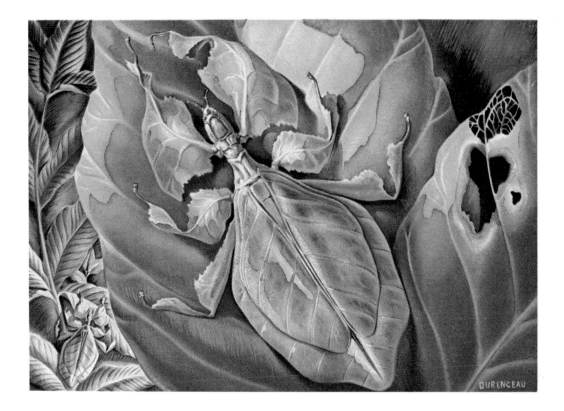

A Leaf That Can Walk

THE Ceylonese walking leaf is a very remarkable insect. Unlike his ferocious cousin, the praying mantis, he is a gentle leaf-eater and has no special equipment with which to defend himself against enemies.

But the walking leaf is usually in little danger of attack.

A tree dweller, his camouflage is one of the most extraordinary found among insects. It protects him in all stages of his existence.

His eggs look exactly like shriveled, spiny seeds. When the young walking leaves emerge, they are wingless, reddish, and glossy, nearly impossible to distinguish from buds at the ends of branches, where they usually feed.

The green body of a full-grown walking leaf is shaped and veined in precise replica of a leaf. The legs are flattened to appear like smaller leaves and are even stained yellow, with ragged edges, as if injured by nibbling insects.

Yet despite this elaborate disguise, the walking leaf has another habit which may serve as an additional precaution for safety. When a wind stirs the tree, he often wiggles himself back and forth in perfect imitation of the agitated leaves.

The Glass Snake

THIS brittle little creature, which snaps off its tail at a touch and then grows a new one, is not a snake at all. It is a lizard, as proved by its ear openings and movable eyelids—characteristics that snakes do not have.

The American glass snake (*Ophisaurus ventralis*) has a variable coloration. Some are black with bright green spots on each scale; others have yellow spots on the scales, which are as highly polished as glass. The animal looks as though it had been freshly varnished.

When the glass snake is handled, the body appears to crack in the tightly fitting armor. If grasped by the tail, it disengages it with a single thrust. No blood appears but the tail thrashes about in a livelier fashion than when attached to the body. While this is going on, the lizard tries to escape; but it has no external legs and moves by stiff lateral undulations of the body quite unlike the sinuous grace of a serpent.

Owls, Rattlesnakes, and Prairie Dogs

PRAIRIE DOGS are not dogs but typical rodents, first cousins to the ground squirrels.

On the treeless western plains and valleys, from North Dakota and Montana to Texas, and thence west across the Rocky Mountains to Utah and Arizona, they are one of the most numerous of animals. Because of their great abundance and their interesting mode of living in colonies, prairie dogs have become one of the most widely known of the smaller mammals. They make their burrows within short distances of each other—only a few yards apart. The inhabitants of these "towns" vary from a few individuals to millions.

In western Texas, one continuous colony is about two hundred fifty miles long and one hundred miles wide. In the entire state of Texas, ninety thousand square miles are occupied by prairie dogs, and the number of animals within this area runs into the hundreds of millions.

Because of the constant danger from coyotes, foxes, and other enemies, the prairie dogs are always on the alert. At the first sign of danger, the town is alive with small scurrying figures rushing for their homes, and the air is filled with a chorus of little barking cries.

It is inevitable that many popular misconceptions should grow up about such numerous and interesting animals. Many people believe that their burrows go down to water, but, like many other desert rodents, these animals do not need to drink. By chemical action in their stomachs, starchy food is transformed into water.

Another popular belief is that rattlesnakes and owls live as a kind of happy family in the burrows of the prairie dogs. The truth is that the ground owls live and breed in deserted dog holes while the rattlesnakes visit the occupied towns to feed on the unfortunate inhabitants.

Sharp Claws Ride on Wings of Velvet

THE great horned owl, "Tiger of the Air," is one of the most savage and powerful of all birds found in America. The incredibly sharp claws can drive through a man's wrist as easily as though they were puncturing tissue paper.

The voice of the great horned owl proclaims "whoo, whoo, whoo." Besides the constant hoot, it utters cries resembling the barking of a dog and the squalling of a child. Sometimes it gives a loud, piercing scream that is one of the most blood-curdling sounds of the deep woods.

Flying with wings as soft as down, it hunts at night, killing rabbits, woodchucks, and occasionally birds as large as turkeys. Domestic cats are not immune, and the owl even attacks skunks without seeming to be affected by their odor. In the North Woods, great horned owls that have been shot were

filled with the quills of a porcupine, an animal usually immune to attack. One owl was found in Massachusetts holding a large blacksnake in his talons with the snake wrapped about his body so that the bird was nearly choked.

In the colder parts of its range, the horned owl nests in February or the first week of March; and in Virginia, as early as late January. The nest is usually the deserted domicile of a hawk or crow, and both male and female incubate the eggs. It lays two eggs, sometimes laying the second one several days after the first. A rather amusing and unscientific inference is that this is done deliberately, so that the one that is hatched first will protect the other yet unhatched egg when the mother bird is away from its nest. Great horned owls are solicitous parents and will attack fearlessly any human that approaches their homes.

As a species, it ranges from the tip of South America north to Central America and Mexico, and to the limit of trees in the far North.

He Carries a Dagger on His Back

THE Caribbean trigger fish (*Balistes vetula*) would end up in the stomach of a shark far oftener than he does except for one thing. He has two sharp spines just behind his head. Normally both spines lie down in shallow grooves along the back, but when the fish is excited or frightened, the forward spine stands up straight while the smaller one behind locks it in place.

The back spine is so strong and heavy that the whole fish can be lifted by it, and no amount of pressure, twisting, or turning will unlock it. The trick is to press down a bit on the smaller spine. Of course the trigger fish can do its own unlocking, but a larger fish who has been foolish enough to swallow a *Balistes* is helpless.

Some trigger fishes have another means of protection. Just behind the pectoral fins, and above the air bladder, is a taut membrane. When the fins are moved rapidly back and forth, the fin-rays strike upon the membrane. This vibrates and acts as a resonator for the underlying air bladder, exactly like the skin of a drum. The noise probably frightens away some enemies, but it may be also a means of communication or a sex call.

How a Desert Plant Meets Its Water Problem

OUR common ragwort, not to be confused with the ragweed of hay fever fame, has this exotic African cousin: *Senecio haworthii.*

Living in an arid land, its chief problem is to arrange for a source of moisture when extra moisture is necessary.

So *Senecio haworthii* has given up some of the common ragwort's wealth of flower, thinness of leaf, and grace of stem in order to develop something quite different. "Leaf succulence," botanists call it. In other words, its leaves become thick, fleshy, and moisture-retaining to provide the plant with a source of extra water in time of need.

This is far from an unusual method of adaptation for plants. The great saguaro cactus of our western deserts does the same thing. Its fluted stem swells during periods of rain, storing up moisture for the dry periods which will surely follow. This is true of many of the other cacti. Travelers in the desert have had their lives saved by cutting open plants to find the accumulated moisture within the stems.

[72]

Adult at Birth

SOME birds intensely dislike housekeeping and the care and feeding of children. Their primary objective, since they must lay eggs, is to get the matter over with as quickly as possible and then forget that it ever happened.

In the Philippines and the Australian region, the Megapode has an exceedingly simple way of disposing of all her domestic problems. Like a reptile, she lays her eggs in a hole in the sand, covers them carefully, and nature takes care of hatching them by means of the heat of the sun. Sometimes the Megapode uses a mound of decaying vegetation for her nest.

Although the bird is about the size of a fowl, her eggs are enormous in proportion to her body—almost as large as goose eggs. After the job of egg-laying is finished, the Megapode pays no more attention to her nest, and

[73]

leaves the children to forage for themselves when they are hatched. Even though they are abandoned before birth, they manage to do very well for themselves, for the fledgling is able to fly almost from the moment of hatching. Otherwise the Megapode would be extinct.

Seals Must be Taught to Swim

SEALS are in a transitory stage, changing from a terrestrial life to a completely aquatic existence. At present they come out on land, or ice, to give birth to their young, and spend only part of their time in the water. If they continue to exist for another million years or so, probably they will become as completely altered in body form and physiological functions as the whales and porpoises.

The hind legs have migrated to the end of the body and appear as finlike flippers; the four limbs are overlaid with tissue to form effective paddles. Like the whales, seals have developed a thick layer of fat, or "blubber," between the skin and the flesh, which acts as a nonconductor and prevents the heat of the body from being absorbed by the water.

The females give birth to their one, or sometimes two, young and nurse them with milk exactly as do other land mammals. Strangely enough, the babies have to be taught to swim. Their mothers toss them in tidepools and keep them there until the squalling little ones learn to paddle and stay afloat.

The animals are divided into two great groups: fur seals and hair seals. The former give the valuable skins of commerce, but the hair seals have comparatively little commercial value, as they lack the soft under-fur which makes the fur seal skins so desirable.

There are many different species of hair seals, living particularly in arctic and northern waters. Their chief enemies, aside from man, are sharks and killer whales; they have continued to exist for thousands of years in their chosen medium where competition is not so great as it would be on land.

The Centipede's Legs

HOW many legs does a centipede have? That depends on which genus of centipede it is, but the number varies from over a score to 173 pairs besides the short feelers. The myriapod (general term for centipede) shown here has forty legs.

While the multiple legs are the centipede's most distinctive feature, it has also other means of protection, which vary in the different species. One common species, *Lithobius mutabilis*, has the habit of feigning death. The type known as *Scolopendridae* includes some species that have four pairs of eyes and some that have no eyes at all. *Scolopendira*, the largest and most important of these, has a poisonous bite dangerous to man. (All centipedes have claws and poison glands used for seizing and killing prey, but only the larger forms can hurt people seriously.)

[75]

The Ship of the Desert

A CAMEL seems to have been made up of spare parts. Nothing could be more grotesque than the long neck, humped body, huge belly, spreading legs, and splay feet.

But if he were not made the way he is, both physiologically and anatomically, he could not exist in the desert. He can drink at one time enough water to last him five or six days. Hard, dry shrubs, bushes, and wirelike grass are the foods he likes best; he would sicken and die with only rich meadow grass to eat. Turn him loose in the desert where a horse or cow would starve, and he is happy. His great belly swells like a balloon and his humps fill with fat. Those are his storage reservoirs. During food shortage, he will draw upon this reserve, and continue to plod across the desert as strongly as though he had had a good meal each night.

His great flat foot-pads act like snow-shoes and carry him over shifting sand, leaving only a slight impression. He will maintain a speed of two-and-one-half miles an hour as regularly as a machine.

The two-humped Bactrian camel lives in Asia. He is a cold weather beast, and grows a heavy coat of wool to protect his body from the icy blasts of the wind across the Gobi Desert. When the temperature drops below the freezing point, he is at his best. Heat almost prostrates him, and the natives let him feed all summer and work only in the winter.

The single-humped dromedary of Africa, on the contrary, loves the blistering sun of the Sahara. His skin is almost naked and he would not live a month in the bitter Gobi cold.

Strangely enough, camels originated in America. Millions of years ago, our western plains swarmed with little camels about the size of sheep, but for some unknown reason, they all left their American homeland and migrated to Asia and Africa. There they thrived and grew, changing as conditions changed to meet their specialized mode of life.

The Greatest Mimics

WARBLERS and finches foraging for insects that feed on rosebushes undoubtedly have a harder time finding the larva of the moth *Amphidasis cognataria* than they do other choice morsels.

For Amphidasis is dressed up like a *rose twig*. His green skin is marked with spots, located and colored like leaf scars, and he holds his slender body at the same angle as the twig he imitates.

To complete the camouflage that foils his foes, Amphidasis has tiny pink forefeet, arranged to form the terminal bud of the twig that he pretends to be.

Insects are the greatest mimics in the entire world of nature. As a rule, the true mimic resembles a conspicuous "model" feared or disliked by its enemies, but some others, like Amphidasis, merely prefer to imitate the surroundings among which they live. Even a bird with his sharp eyesight may fail to penetrate its disguise.

The Ape That Walks Like a Man

NATURE has made the gorilla almost a ground-living ape. Because of its great weight, the beast cannot easily climb about among the trees as do the chimpanzee and the orangutang. Therefore it spends much of its time on all fours, like a huge baboon in the thick vegetation of the African jungle.

The gorilla's long forearms are enormously powerful but its short hind legs are comparatively weak. Nevertheless, it can walk erect and even run for a short distance.

The gorilla is a terrifying beast and seems to know it. If an intruder surprises it, the great ape will rise up and pound its breast, growling in a most horrifying manner, and then lunge forward. This seems to be a bluff, for if the enemy does not run, the beast often stops short, drops to the ground, and moves away.

The big ape has few natural enemies, for any other animal would think twice before coming within range of the powerful arms and long canine teeth. Even a lion might emerge second-best in a fight with a full-grown gorilla. The popular legend of native women being carried off by gorillas is pure fantasy.

New York Zoological Society

The Tree-Climbing Fish

IN the mangrove swamps of North Borneo lives a strange little fish only a few inches long. It is called *Periophthalmus,* the mud skipper, or tree-climbing fish, one of the most remarkable of nature's freaks. The fish spends most of its time hopping about the mud flats in search of food or basking in the sun. It even climbs out of the water up on mangrove roots or stones when in pursuit of victims.

While out of the water the large gill chambers are kept filled with air and the tail is often left hanging down in the water. It literally breathes through the skin of the tail more efficiently than by means of gills. It can survive for thirty-six hours with its tail submerged but hardly half that long if only the gills are allowed to function. It has become so accustomed to a life out of the water that it is unable to live in what should be its native element for any length of time.

Besides the breathing tail, this fish has developed another unique feature —flexible, magnified vision. Its movable, bulbous eyes are adjustable to vision in the air as well as in the water. A special muscle enables the fish to shift the spherical lens so close to the retina as to produce a sharp image even of objects at some distance.

The Champion Lightweight Fighter of the Mammal World

THE pigmy shrew is one of the smallest mammals in the world, but despite its minute size, it has terrific courage and ferocity, and without hesitation will attack and kill mice and rats many times its own weight.

The common shrew measures about four inches in total length and weighs only four ounces. The body is slender, the nose long and sharp, and the ears hardly discernible in the dense fur. On each side of the body, between the elbow and the knee, there is a gland which secretes a peculiar and odorous fluid—especially strong during the mating season.

It eats insects, larvae, worms, and any kind of obtainable flesh. Every day, winter and summer, the shrew consumes three-fourths as much as his body weight, and because of the speed with which he digests food, he cannot skip many meals without disaster. Therefore, he is always on the move, and is equally active by day or night, running about debris on the ground or in holes beneath the surface.

His small eyes are of little value, but the long flexible snout is used constantly, and is the main reliance of the little beast not only to catch his prey but for information as to the outside world.

The common shrew is a solitary animal of so morose a disposition that if two are placed in a cage together they almost immediately go into furious combat, and the victor devours the body of his companion at a single meal.

Shrews are circumpolar in distribution—ranging through England, Asia, and North America as far south as Guatemala.

Why the Yucca Moth Is a Model Parent

THIS North American moth (*Tegeticula alba*), which lives on the yucca plant, has a very ingenious method of providing for her offspring. When the time for egg-laying comes, this moth climbs deep into the flower of the yucca plant, carrying a mass of pollen gathered from other yuccas.

Afterwards she carefully thrusts more pollen into the flower. By doing this, she makes sure that the plant is fertilized and that the yucca seeds will develop as her eggs are hatched. Regardless of what happens to her, there will be an ample supply of food for the children.

Kick and Run

THE dodo became extinct because it had lost the use of its wings by disuse and had developed no other means of protection. The ostrich, too, is a bird which cannot lift its great body into the air by its weak wings, and therefore has become completely grounded. But nature has given it such long, powerful legs that it can race over the plains as fast as a horse. Moreover, if an enemy approaches too closely, the bird will leap at it fiercely, striking right and left with its feet, and the sharp claws can rake an animal's body like knives. A kick from an ostrich is no laughing matter, as more than one African native has discovered. The bird depends for its protection almost entirely upon alertness, speed, and its fighting ability, for an ostrich on the African veldt is a most conspicuous object.

The female makes her nest on the open plains, but when she is sitting on the eggs, she stretches out her neck flat upon the ground, thus giving a certain measure of concealment. If an enemy approaches too near, both parents will run toward it endeavoring to entice the intruder away from the nest.

Ostrich eggs are not only very good eating, but one egg makes a substantial meal.

True ostriches are found only in Africa, but during the Ice Age, perhaps fifty thousand years ago, a giant species, known as *Struthiolithes*, lived in China and on the Mongolian plateau. The huge fossil eggs found in the yellow earth of North China are not rare in curio shops.

A Fish Hitchhiker

THE sucking fish, remora, is a hitchhiker of the first water, always catching a ride on a whale, a shark, or a manta and contributing nothing whatever to the comfort or enjoyment of its host. When a shark has snapped up another fish, the remora releases himself and feeds on the floating bits of the shark's meal. Then he catches up with his host again and rides on to the next feeding station. That is not all!

If the remora is frightened, it actually darts into the shark's mouth for protection and fastens itself on the gum just behind the teeth. The shark's tongue is relatively immobile, and it is impossible for it to bite or detach its uninvited guest until he is ready to leave. More often the remora goes into the shark's gill chamber and remains safely invisible until the danger is over. Thus the remora, although rendering no service to his host, gets a ride, food, and protection all free.

Some of these sucking fish are eight or ten inches long but others reach a length of only two or three inches.

He Can Fly Backward

*H*UMMERS are the only birds in the world that can fly backward; moreover, they are the smallest existing feathered creatures. The tiniest of them all is Helena's hummingbird, only two and one half inches in length with a bill less than one half inch long. It is true that hummers like the nectar of flowers, but when one plumbs the depth of a corolla, it is not only to taste its sweets; the tiny flies, bees, beetles, and spiders in the cup are just as acceptable to the little bird's stomach. After the nutriment has been extracted from the bodies of insects, the indigestible parts are formed into minute pellets and regurgitated. Although flowers are attractive to most hummingbirds, some forest-inhabiting species pay little attention to blossoms but glean the moss-covered bark of the trees searching for animal food. Others feed on gnats whirling about in the air. The hummers hang with rapidly vibrating wings, seizing the tiny insects, one by one, in flight.

Hummingbirds are often confused with the equally large sphinx moths which in the evening hover over beds of petunias and other flowers, and probe their cups exactly as do the little birds.

The ruby-throat's nest is made from soft plant downs, formed into a cup-shaped structure, placed firmly on a twig or branch. The outside is covered with bits of bark and moss bound in place with spider web. It resembles a knot or excrescence so closely that only the sharpest eyes can discover it. A masterful bit of camouflage.

Although the ruby-throat is the only hummer east of the Mississippi River, approximately four hundred eighty-eight species are known, ranging from the tip of South America to Canada and Alaska. They live only in the New World.

The Frog With a Built-in Food Supply

FOR the Amazonian tree frog (*Hyla resinifictrix*) building a home is the hardest part of raising a family.

The frog selects a hollow in a tree trunk, situated so as to catch the rain. Then it waterproofs the cavity by lining it with beeswax from the comb of a friendly species of bee found abundantly in the jungle.

Once the beeswax bowl is filled with rainwater, Hyla lays her eggs—and the job of bringing up the young is practically done. For not only does the young family have a snug home, but each pollywog is born with its own food supply: *an extra-fleshy tail*. As the young change from tadpoles to frogs, their tails are absorbed to furnish nutriment for growing bodies. And until they're able to hop about and rustle up their own meals, they need no other food.

The Origin of "Playing Possum"

NEWLY born opossums are formless, naked little objects so firmly attached to the teats in their mother's pouch that they cannot be shaken loose. Later, when they attain a coating of hair, they continue to occupy the pouch until they become too large for it. Then they crawl out and cluster all over their mother's body, hanging onto her thick fur with their little feet.

There is a widespread belief that the mother arches her tail over her back like a rail and that the young ride "picaback," hanging onto it with their little prehensile tails. Probably this does happen at times, but certainly it is very rare. An opossum, especially when climbing about among the branches, is constantly using its tail as a balance and would be hindered greatly by having a family attached to it.

Opossums are rather slow-moving, stupid animals which seek safety by their retiring, nocturnal habits and non-resistance to enemies. It is because of this last trait that the familiar phrase, "playing possum," originated. If a 'possum is cornered, he will often stand with hanging head and tail and half-closed eyes. If he is pushed over, he will lie flat and limp, apparently dead. If one tries to raise him and put him on his feet, he will show not the slightest signs of life.

Opossums are the only American members of the ancient order of marsupials, the pouch animals, that live in Australasia. In the New England states they seem to be working their way farther northward every year, and now are found as far up as Vermont.

Black Star

How The Australian Sea Horse Escapes Notice

ONE of the most fantastic of all marine creatures is the Australian sea horse or sea dragon (*Phyllopteryx eques*).

His home is among the waving seaweeds on the coral banks of Indo-Pacific waters. About ten inches long when fully grown, he is small in comparison with many of his enemies. He has no means of defense. And, because of the upright position in which he carries himself, he is a very poor swimmer. He cannot escape by flight.

With these handicaps, the sea dragon would long ago have become extinct were it not for his remarkable protective camouflage and the convenient prehensile tail which enables him to make this camouflage effective.

Long, leafy appendages extend from his body. In shape, color, and texture these appendages so closely resemble his seaweed habitat that it is almost impossible to distinguish the fish from the plant, once he has hooked himself to it by means of his unique tail.

Anchored thus, he is safe from the treacherous currents that might sweep him from his hiding place out into full view of his enemies. In this way he usually manages to escape notice.

The Fastest Animal

FOR a short dash, a cheetah, or hunting leopard, can reach a speed of seventy miles an hour. The animal is particularly adapted for running, having long legs, slender body, and narrow chest. Cheetahs know, of course, that they have no chance with an antelope or with a gazelle in a long race, so they lie in concealment until their prey is near enough to be caught in a short flying dash.

In India, cheetahs are used by the princes for capturing black buck, a common antelope of the plains. The beasts are kept chained until a short distance from the prey, when they are released and give a spectacular exhibition of speed.

The spotted coat, like that of the leopard and jaguar, blends so completely with the light and shadow of the leaves and grass in the jungle that it acts as a splendid camouflage.

Cheetahs are found only in Africa and India.

Sharks Do Bite

DO sharks attack humans? You may be very sure they do; and even if you are a "doubting Thomas," you had better not go swimming when large sharks are about. Most sharks feed on flesh of some kind, and the mere fact that it is human flesh is neither here nor there—it tastes as good to them.

Sharks, as a rule, will not attack living, active, large mammals unless they are very hungry or get the smell of blood. But the great white shark (*Charodon*), which has existed since early geological times, is as savage as a tiger, and will kill anything that moves in the waters of its habitat.

The biggest of all the species, the great whale shark, although it reaches a length of sixty feet, is absolutely harmless, for its teeth are not adapted to eat large food.

Although most sharks live in salt water, a few species have changed their physiology so that they can be happy in the mouths of rivers or in fresh water lakes. *Carcharis nicaraguenis* is one of them. He inhabits Lake Nicaragua, and is a real menace to the natives who happen to fall in the water, for no one will go in purposely. He is a big shark, eight feet long, very active and ferocious.

For the most part, sharks bring forth their young alive. The remainder, however, produce eggs which are nearly always enclosed in a curious, oblong protective case, often provided with horns or tendrils at the corners.

Dancing Fiddler

THE cricket is one of the saltatorial insects—he gets around by leaping or dancing, and he is content to fiddle his way through life.

His instrument is very simple—a toothed fiddlestick and vibrating tympanums. The five hundred prisms of the bow, biting on the ridges of the wing cover opposed to it, set all four tympanums vibrating at once—the lower pair by direct friction, the upper pair by vibrations of the wing cover itself. One cannot be sure why the cricket fiddles. Perhaps it is just because he is a happy little fellow with a buoyant spirit; perhaps it communicates some kind of intelligence such as recognition, sex calls, or danger signals.

The cricket always must be on the watch for enemies, particularly lizards and ants. The ant falls upon the baby cricket, eviscerates and then devours it.

The great French naturalist, M. Fabre, tells us that the field cricket (*Gryllus campestris*), as he grows older, yearns to become a solid citizen, a fellow with a permanent address. So, after a brief, irresponsible youth, he settles down. Choosing a spot with a good sunny exposure, he starts to dig. He makes a small house first. But he keeps improving it—deepening his hall, enlarging his bedroom, making a clean-swept doorway where he can sit and strum away on summer evenings. And, invariably, his doorway is concealed under a tuft of grass which protects it from intruders.

The Giraffe's Extension Ladder

THE giraffe that lived millions of years ago was a forest-dwelling creature like the present-day okapi. Nature helped the giraffe in two
extraordinary ways. It gave it protective coloration for concealment in the
forests, and amazing height so that it could enjoy, as food, the leaves on the
upper branches of trees. A full-grown giraffe is more than eighteen feet
high, and much of that height is its "extension ladder" neck, which the ani-

mal developed when its legs had grown as long as they could without becoming detrimental or fragile.

But the giraffe was not content to live in the forest. It moved out of the forest into the plains and now it goes only to the edge of the woods to feed. Out in the open its coloration is far from effective for concealment. Its long neck is not a hindrance but it is no longer quite so helpful as it was. The present-day giraffe counts on its long legs for protection: they're astonishingly speedy and their kicks are vicious. Giraffes are confined to Africa.

The World's Oldest Living Animal

HERE is now on St. Helena a tortoise from Aldabra that was on that island when Napoleon was there more than a century ago. How old this tortoise was when brought to St. Helena we do not know. But venerable as it seems, its age is exceeded by that of another tortoise which is living on the island of Mauritius. In 1810 it was specifically mentioned as a national possession in the treaty by which the French ceded Mauritius to England. It was said to have lived there seventy years previously so it is safe to conclude that it is about two hundred years old. These historic tortoises have attained the greatest ages *recorded* for any animals, being the oldest known members of an ancient and long lived race, for even such little species as our box turtle reaches a good old age.

Tortoises go back far into the geological past and seem to have changed very little with the passing of time. Even those of forty million years ago looked almost like the living animals of today.

The first "armored tank" was the tortoise, and its curious armor accounts in large degree for its amazingly long life. Obviously, the hard shell affords protection while permitting mobility—without speed, it is true. But the tortoise's slowness may very well be a big factor in its longevity, for its organs won't wear out so fast, not being subject to the strains of more active animals.

Champion Glider

THE man of war, or frigate, bird is a genuine feathered airplane. Without moving its wings for hours at a time, it floats high in the air ascending in spirals or drifting lazily along, directing its easy flight by changes of the angle of its "planes" so slightly that any such effort is not apparent.

The bird is very impressive by reason of its size and the enormous stretch of its wings measuring seven and a half feet across. When a flock of thousands of individuals soar on motionless pinions, they look like an aerial army of invasion.

At sundown they roost in bushes or mangrove trees by the shore, but their weak and clumsy feet make it difficult for them to take off from anything except a high place.

It is strictly a tropical bird, seldom being seen farther north than the coasts of Florida and southern California.

The Salamander That Wouldn't Grow Up

FOR a long time it seemed impossible for naturalists to admit that an animal which lives for years without losing its gills, and is able to propagate in that state, could be anything but a perfect form. But the axolotl proved them wrong.

Technically, he isn't a finished product of any ordinary life cycle. He is simply the aquatic larva of the North American salamander (*Ambystoma tigrinum*), and he has the ability to adjust himself to changes in his living conditions that might cause a lot of us humans to turn green with envy.

His parent form, *Ambystoma*, leaves the water after complete metamorphosis, the last stage of which is marked by the loss of gills.

Down Mexico way, and in some of our western lakes, the axolotl finds a veritable paradise in the place where he was born. He has a constant abundance of food, a stable amount of water, and fine hiding spots under banks. There is nothing whatever to prevent him from leaving the lakes, but nothing to induce him to do so, since he couldn't possibly better his living conditions. So the creature remains a half-finished product without changing into the adult condition.

The Mexicans have known the axolotl from remotest times, and use it as a favorite food although it is only eleven inches long. Its name was given to it by the Aztecs long before white men came to Mexico.

Porpoises Once Lived on Land

IT seems incredible that many millions of years ago whales and their relatives, the porpoises, actually lived on land and walked on four legs. Their long slender bodies, pointed heads, and finlike flippers give them such a fishlike appearance that even today many people do not realize that they are true land mammals.

A porpoise or a whale must hold its breath when it is below the surface and would drown were it submerged too long. The nostrils in most porpoises are semicircular openings on the top of the head. They are tightly closed the moment the beast dives. As soon as the animal appears at the surface, it blows out its highly heated breath which condenses in the colder air and forms a column of steam or spray; thus the popular idea that the animal takes water in through the mouth and blows it out through the nose.

Porpoises, like whales, give birth to their young alive, nurse them with milk, and have warm blood as do other mammals.

At the aquarium, "Marineland," near St. Augustine, Florida, porpoises were captured and transferred to the great tank. Here they live happily and have shown that they can be domesticated easily under such ideal conditions. They evince considerable intelligence and great affection for their young.

Why the porpoises took up a completely aquatic existence and thus drastically changed their physiology and anatomy, is an unsolved question, but they could never have existed in water if they had not learned to hold their breath by closing their nostrils.

The Bird That Swings and Sways

PERHAPS you know him as the "thunder bird," perhaps as the "pump handler," but a bittern by any name is still a master of camouflage. Not only is his body colored like the reeds among which he lives, but he passes himself off as a cattail. If a hawk or other enemy approaches, he stands with his body stiff and upright, his head pointed to the sky. Even when a wind rustles the cattails and sets them nodding, the bittern clings to his tricky disguise. As the reeds start swinging, he begins to swing from side to side with the same motion—first with his neck and head, and then with his whole body. He knows well enough that he is virtually invisible, and will let you pass within a few feet of him without taking wing.

He is a lover of boggy marshes where he stands in solitude concealed by the rushes, and spends much of his time looking for frogs and small fish.

The bittern is famous for peculiar notes heard chiefly in the breeding season, but sometimes in the autumn. These are compared to the sound produced by working a wooden pump, and to that of a stick being struck by an axe. No one knows exactly how or why these sounds are produced; but they are accompanied by violent contortions of the bird's head and neck.

Naturalists know him as *Botaurus lentiginosus*. He breeds from British Columbia to Newfoundland and south as far as Florida.

Scarecrows Don't Scare Crows

WERE the crow not such a remarkably clever bird, it could not have existed in such numbers where it is a continual object of attack by man. Farmers who try to keep crows away from their corn by the use of "scarecrows" find the birds virtually laughing at man's feeble attempts to frighten them. Yet the crow is exceedingly wary. He seems to be able to judge the range of a rifle to a nicety, but his ability to survive is due in large measure to the fact that he never takes chances. For example, when a flock of crows is feeding in a cornfield, two or three of their number act as sentries, stationed on fence posts or tall trees. A cry of warning from one of their sentries will send the whole flock winging away to safety.

The crow is commonly regarded as a blackleg and a thief. He does pull up sprouting corn, destroy chickens, and rob the nests of smaller birds; but he also eats toads, frogs, and a good deal of insect food such as predaceous beetles. Therefore, he can not be considered all bad by any means.

Crows make very amusing pets and furnish endless amusement for their owners. They always display a thieving propensity amounting to what would be called kleptomania in human beings. They have a passion for stealing and hiding any shining object of a bright color such as scissors or thimbles.

His Nose Is An Arm

THE elephant's trunk is one of the most extraordinary adaptations by nature for a specialized life. It is an elongated nose, but the elephant uses it as one would a hand or an arm. With the sensitive tip, the animal can pick up a peanut or a log weighing several hundred pounds with equal facility. He uses it to scent an enemy, to spray water over his back while taking a bath, and as a weapon of defense. A blow from an elephant's trunk could crush a man.

Another extraordinary provision for the elephant's unusual mode of life is the great ivory tusks. They are useful not only for fighting weapons but in a dozen different ways to get the animal's food.

His sense of smell is extremely acute and his hearing is good, but his eyesight is weak. The elephant has virtually no enemies except man.

It is agreed, universally, that of all big game animals, elephants most resemble human beings in family life and habits; it is also agreed that much of their remarkable intelligence is due to their superior memory. Hundreds of anecdotes are told to prove that an elephant never forgets. Although many of these stories are embroidered with fiction, still there are dozens of proved instances where captive elephants have, after many years, rewarded a past kindness with affection or treachery with revenge.

It seems almost inconceivable that so huge an animal could possibly be difficult to discern. Nevertheless, when an elephant is standing motionless amid leaves and branches in the half-gloom of a tropical jungle, it is nearly invisible except to a trained eye. Moreover, elephants can move through the tangle of a thick forest almost as noiselessly as a cat treading on a soft rug.

Elephants are native only to Africa and Asia.

Black Star

His Nose Is His Protection

THE aptness of the name "white tail" for the Virginia deer (*Odocoileus virginianus*) is obvious to anyone who has startled a deer in the forest. Off it goes in leaps of from fifteen to twenty feet, with the tail upright, flashing white danger signals at every jump. Nature has given the white tail deer marvelous hearing and scent to protect it from enemies, but its eyesight is not the best. It seems to regard all motionless objects downwind as features of the landscape.

The adults have two strongly contrasted coats each year—brownish-gray in the winter and reddish-brown in summer. The red pelage is conspicuous but the deer depends upon the heavy foliage to protect it from sight. During the winter when the leaves are gone, the counter-shaded dark body blends perfectly with the bushes and branches.

The spotted coat of the fawn and its deathlike stillness are wonderful safeguards. The baby is left in the forest-cover for a month or more by the mother, and hardly moves during that time.

The deer that live in the North face grave danger during the winter months, for the heavy snows make food scarce and travel difficult. Their small, sharp hooves and slim legs sink deep into the snow with each step. Instinct, however, provides deer with a way to obtain food under these adverse conditions. They gather together in parties in dense growth where food is plentiful, remaining throughout the season and forming a "yard" by keeping a network of hard-beaten paths open through the snow in order to reach the browse afforded by the bushes and trees.

The fact that white tails are still abundant over much of North America is eloquent testimony to the safeguards nature has given them.

Why Chuckwalla Wears an Oversize Skin

THE chuckwalla lizard (*Sauromalus ater*) lives among the sun-baked rock ledges of the southwest deserts. He needs a very high temperature else he refuses to eat, and will literally starve to death.

Chuckwalla is no sleek beauty. He is of a dull, rusty-brown color that harmonizes perfectly with the desert sand; his tough, scaly hide sags about his body in loose folds which gives him a sluggish, ungainly appearance. But while Chuckwalla's draped skin doesn't help his looks, it does aid him in escaping his enemies. When he is taking a sun bath on a burning-hot rock, and a desert hawk appears in the brassy sky, Chuckwalla scrambles to the nearest ledge crevice and tumbles in. Then his slack hide gives him plenty of room to blow himself up, until his skin scales press against the rock walls. Thus anchored, the strongest claws can't drag him from his refuge. What method of defense could be more ingenious?

Will the Zebra Change His Stripes?

THE zebra—like the giraffe, described earlier—presents an unusual aspect of nature's protective system. For its unique defensive device is not only no longer valuable, but also it is now somewhat disadvantageous.

The zebra's stripes served their camouflaging purpose in the time, millions of years ago, when the zebra was a smaller creature, living in the forests. The stripes that make this animal so conspicuous when seen at close range were very effective for concealment at a distance and under forest light-and-shade conditions.

But for some reason the zebra took to the plains. There its protective coloration device was insufficient and it could never have survived in the open without the other arrows to its bow—great speed and fine senses of sight and smell.

It would seem that for the zebra in its current plains type of existence the stripes, if not actually a hindrance, are no longer necessary. But protective devices are not easily or quickly discarded. And in many animals you can see the equivalent of these stripes that have apparently outlived their usefulness.

He Wears an Armor of Moss

NATURE has done some remarkable things in adapting animals to a specialized way of living, but she really went all out in the case of the tree sloth.

Instead of walking or crawling on all fours, the sloth spends his life upside down—hanging from the limbs of trees. He can't stand upright on four legs like an ordinary beast. Moreover, instead of having a coat to match his home in the dense tropical forest, his long coarse hair is actually encrusted with a peculiar green alga which closely resembles lichen on the trees. He is virtually invisible in the thick jungle.

The sloth certainly has need of special protection, for he is helpless to defend himself against enemies like eagles and tree-climbing jaguars. He cannot run away, for he is restricted to inching along slowly on the under side of a branch by means of his strongly hooked claws.

During the day he sleeps hanging with all four feet close together and head drawn up between his four legs. In this position, he looks exactly like the stump of a lichen-covered bough. And one might almost touch him without realizing that he is a living, breathing animal.

His formal name is the three-toed sloth (*Bradypus tridactylus*), and he lives in the densest part of the South American forests.

The King of Birds

THE bald eagle is a true "king of birds," whether he is soaring and circling far above the earth or plunging like a meteor from the sky; screaming defiance at the storm or fiercely striking his prey, he is the embodiment of pride, power and courage.

After six years of debate, the bald eagle was finally adopted as our national emblem by the Congress on June 20, 1782, although Benjamin Franklin strongly favored the wild turkey.

Nature has given the eagle wonderful eyesight, great speed on the wing, and talons so powerful that even if it were wounded and cornered, a large animal would hesitate to attack it. Because it is supreme in the air and has no natural enemies, the eagle makes no attempt at concealment either for itself or its huge nest, usually perching on dead branches in full view of the world.

Fish is its favorite food and it is seldom found far from water. Sometimes it will plunge from a great height, descending at an acute angle, and go beneath the surface after a fish. It often robs the smaller osprey, or so-called "fish hawk," of its prey. Attacked in mid-air, the osprey will drop its fish, and the eagle swoops down with lightning speed, catching it before it strikes the water.

Eagles sometimes kill even large birds, including ducks, coots, and geese, but as a rule these are crippled, or sick, individuals. The eagle will also attack lambs and foxes, but the legend of eagles carrying babies off to their nests has never been substantiated and is probably pure fiction.

Bald eagles mate for life and have a strong home-loving instinct. There is a record of a pair of eagles, or their successors, that occupied one nest in

Ohio for thirty-five years without a break. When the tree was finally destroyed in a storm, the birds selected another site only a short distance away in the same grove and continued to raise their families until it, too, was blown down.

An Elder Statesman of the Bird World

EXCEPT for vultures and parrots, wild geese live longer than any other birds. Authentic records give them as much as seventy years. Geese mate for life and show extraordinary devotion to each other. After a pair have become mutually attracted, they carry on a platonic existence for two and sometimes three years, apparently having a trial marriage to be certain their personalities are congenial. When, at last, they make up their minds to set up housekeeping, the nest may be put in any one of a most amazing variety of places. In western regions it is sometimes found on high cliffs, or even in trees near the water where osprey nests are available. Often the female utilizes the top of a muskrat house. But the nest is always in a spot where the old geese can use their wonderful eyesight, hearing, and inherited caution to protect themselves from enemies. Probably no other bird except the wild turkey is as clever and successful in avoiding possible enemies.

When the young are born, they take to the water immediately, and swim like veterans on the first try. At an alarm note from the mother, the goslings will dive, swim under water, and reach the cover of reeds or bushes. They have even been known to hold to rushes and stones to help keep themselves submerged, sticking their bills above the surface to breathe. The birds range from the Yukon across the continent to Labrador. They winter as far south as Florida and Mexico, and as far north as British Columbia.

The Fish with an Electric Fence

IT sounds like a "fish story" to say that a fish four feet in length and only five or six inches in diameter can generate an electric current several times more powerful than that of an ordinary automobile, and yet the electric eel can do just that.

Drs. C. W. Coates and Robert T. Cox found by experiments that an eel three feet long attains a maximum of 450 to 600 volts. The electric current applied for household use is 110 volts, and a standard electric lamp is about 60 watts. Experiments on an electric eel have drawn 600 volts and about 1,000 watts which is obviously enough to light many electric bulbs. The discharges are strong enough to knock down, and perhaps kill, a horse and it is no safer for man or beast to come in contact with them than to run into an uninsulated electric wire.

The electricity is generated in glands. These organs begin behind the head and extend nearly the whole length of its cylindrical body. The skin and other tissues surrounding the generators are electricity conductors.

Swimming about in the warm waters of the Amazon and Orinoco Rivers, of South America, the eels obtain food by stunning the other fish upon which they feed. Moreover they protect themselves from the swarming, incredibly savage piranhas by building an invisible electric fence that no creature of the jungle rivers can penetrate.

The Insect Tiger With the Knifelike Limbs

PROBABLY no other insect is the subject of so many widespread legends as is the praying mantis. The Greeks endowed it with supernatural powers. Arabs believe that it prays continually with its face turned toward Mecca, and the Nubians held it in great esteem. The Hottentots believe that if it alights on any person, it is a sign of that person's saintliness. But the praying mantis is far from a saint; rather, he is the tiger of the insect world. Its green color conceals it from enemies as well as from its prey.

The forepair of limbs are peculiarly modified, the strong third joint bearing on its curved under side a channel armed on each edge with strong movable spines. Into this groove the stout second joint, its sharp edge adapted for cutting, can close like the blade of a penknife. A praying mantis waits for prey in its characteristic devotional attitude or stalks it with slow and silent movements, finally seizing it with its knifelike blades, and devours it. The mantis eats flies, insects, and caterpillars; the large South American species even attacks lizards, frogs, and birds.

All of them are pugnacious fighters with their swordlike limbs and the loser is frequently devoured. The Chinese match them like fighting cocks. Sometimes females eat their husbands.

From a painting by Grohe

What Really Happens to Swallows in the Winter?

OR hundreds of years nobody in England knew what happened to the common swallow (*Hirundo rustica*) in the wintertime. Some thought that they made a hole in soft mud and went to sleep for the winter, like turtles.

Samuel Johnson had this to say about it: "Swallows certainly sleep all the winter. A number of them conglobulate together, by flying round and round, and then all in a heap throw themselves under water and lie in the bed of a river."

At last, in the nineteenth century, English naturalists found out what really happens to swallows. The birds fly south to Africa for the winter. They go in small groups of from thirty to fifty birds instead of in the large flocks in which they are seen just before migration. These small groups of small birds become indiscernible almost as soon as they start southward.

Why the Puff Adder Should Be Called the Bluff Adder

THE most consummate actor in the reptilian world is the puff adder, or hog-nose snake (*Heterodon contortrix*). He is a completely harmless serpent and he knows it, so he stages an act in front of an enemy that is most effective, and yet ludicrous to a human.

His body is short and thick, his markings not unlike some rattlers. Altogether he is a rather terrifying-looking snake.

If you corner him, he puts up a tremendous bluff. He flattens and widens his head until it assumes a most formidable triangular outline, rears up, hisses, and makes a feint at striking. If you don't scare, he tries another performance. He appears to be attacked by convulsions. He writhes in agony with head twisted to one side, mouth gaping open with the tongue lolling out, and sometimes drawing part of his body through his open jaws. After further contortions the reptile rolls upon his back.

It is a fine piece of acting in simulating death agonies, and everything is perfect except the snake's insistence on remaining on his back. If rolled over on his stomach, he will immediately turn upon his back again.

If you hide and watch, pretty soon he will begin to show signs of life, look about, and if no one is in evidence, he will start to wriggle off as fast as he can.

The hog-nose snake is common from Massachusetts to Florida and west to Minnesota and Texas.

He is sometimes known as the flat-headed adder, the hissing adder, and other names in keeping with his antics.

The Fish With the Anti-Aircraft Gun

THE archer fish (*Toxotes jaculator*) is a small fish with a flashing yellow and black-barred body, and with unusual tastes. He is not content, like most small fish, to eat the shrimp or insect larvae which swarm in the streams and ponds of Thailand and other East Indian countries where he lives.

He insists on something extra. His favorite food is flying insects. And he has an extraordinary way of bringing these delicacies within reach, since he has no means of going after them—he shoots them down with water flak.

He waits just beneath the surface of the water until a tempting insect settles on some overhanging twig or perhaps flies overhead. Then, pushing his mouth upward, he shoots his liquid charge straight at his quarry. Battered and wet, the insect falls into the water and is quickly swallowed.

The Valhalla of the Johnny Penguins

PENGUINS are completely flightless birds, with wings overlaid with skin to form effective paddles and with feet so far at the end of their bodies that they can move on land only by standing erect. Why this bird forsook the air we do not know, but it has equipped itself in this way for successful existence on land and sea.

One of the strangest and most romantic stories about penguins is told by Dr. Robert Cushman Murphy of the American Museum of Natural History. At South Georgia Island in the subantarctic, Dr. Murphy observed that he almost never found the dead bodies of full-grown Johnny penguins. One day, while on a coastal hill south of the Bay of Isles, he discovered the reason. He came suddenly upon a little transparent lake formed entirely of snow water. Around its margins stood several sickly Johnny penguins, silent and drooping. They seemed completely exhausted by the toilsome climb from the beach to the top of the hill.

"I don't know why," said he, "but the air seemed oppressed with tragedy —there was a sense of invisible drama. It seemed strange that none of the penguins that went into the pond ever came out again, so I walked to the rim of the pool and looked into its translucent depths. On the cold blue bottom, with their flippers outstretched, were hundreds, possibly thousands, of dead Johnny penguins that had made their last weary climb up the hill to reach this peaceful spot. Safe from their terrible enemies, the sea leopard, and from the skua gulls in the air, they had come to their last rest."

Dr. Murphy tells another, and more cheerful, story of the Johnny penguin. He says that their love-making follows a very rigid pattern. When a male Johnny proposes to the damsel of his heart, he selects a pebble and lays it at his sweetheart's feet with pride and affection. If the lady penguin picks it up, they are engaged. If she doesn't care for the gentleman in the same way, she leaves the stone untouched. Then he picks it up again, walks away, and eventually offers it to another penguin girl. One old Johnny waddled up to Dr. Murphy and gravely laid at his feet the shiny top of a condensed milk can. The curator picked it up, bowed deeply to the penguin, and they parted with mutual expressions of respect and esteem.

The several species of penguins are confined to the southern latitudes, mostly in the subantarctic and antarctic region. The great Emperor penguin, so beloved by antarctic explorers, is the largest of the group.

The Bird That Cannot Fly

THE kiwi bird of New Zealand is permanently grounded, for he has no wings. But unlike the dodo, which also could not fly, it has been able to exist because nature provided it with other means of protection.

The kiwi is about the size of a fowl, dark reddish-brown with longitudinal stripes and cross-bars of black.

He is entirely nocturnal and sleeps throughout the day, but when twilight comes, he moves about as cautiously and noiselessly as a rat. His powerful legs enable him to get over the ground with long strides at an extraordinary rate, and, if annoyed, he strikes with such force and rapidity that his long claws become dangerous weapons.

The kiwi's long bill reminds one of the woodcock, for it is highly sensitive. Worms are its principal food. The kiwi drives its flexible bill into the ground to feel about for them. If it finds one, the bird draws the worm out with extreme care, coaxing it, as it were, by degrees, instead of pulling roughly and breaking it; then the kiwi throws back its head and swallows the morsel whole. When looking for its food or exploring the ground, the bird makes a continuous sniffing sound through its nostrils, which are at the very tip of its bill, and touches every object, but he is probably guided more by touch than by smell.

The kiwi was discovered in 1813, but was supposed to be some sort of a hoax and was not definitely determined, by naturalists, to exist until some years later.

The First Snorkel

ACCORDING to geological records the phytosaur is one of the first known residents of the New York City area. He lived about two hundred million years ago in what geologists call the Triassic period. A reptile about twelve feet in length, he had a curious beaklike snout armed with sharp teeth.

The phytosaur was a crawler and a swimmer. In many ways he resembled our modern crocodile. But he differed in two important respects. His nostrils were set back near his eyes instead of at the end of his snout. And the teeth at the tip of his snout were long and curved like nippers on a pair of tongs.

The phytosaur was equipped in this strange way for a very good reason. With his nostrils so far back, he could float along just under the surface of the water with just the top of his head protruding, and thus sneak up on his unsuspecting prey.

The Tricky Road Runner

SNAKE eater, lizard bird, cock of the desert, war bird, ground cuckoo, medicine bird, road runner, chapparal bird, *pisano*—all mean the same bird, *Geococcyx californianus*. These different names express to some degree the picturesque and fascinating personality of Mr. G. californianus.

G. californianus is a useful and amusing citizen, notable for his canny devices. Down in the Southwest, the natives swear by him; and New Mexico has even adopted him as the state bird. That he does kill and eat rattlesnakes is beyond doubt. He digests rapidly, but when he starts eating a two-foot snake, he may go around for hours with part of it dangling from his mouth until digestive juices have had time to act. Mr. Frank Dobie reports that a friend saw a road runner kill a rattlesnake three and a half feet long. The fight was in a cow pen. With wings extended and dragging in the dust, the bird would run at the snake, aiming at its head. The rattler struck blindly several times, hitting the road runner's wings. Finally the snake was exhausted and the bird leaped on its back, pecked a hole in the snake's skull, and punctured the brain. It ate the brain but nothing else.

In the West it is widely believed, perhaps erroneously, that the road runner builds a little corral of cholla cactus spines around a sleeping rattler and that the snake kills himself by frantically slashing against the cholla. It is true, however, that the road runner is a very resourceful bird and that it carries snail shells to a rock and dashes them apart on it with a swift stroke of the head in order to eat the contents. This performance has even been photographed. That he might build a cactus corral about a sleeping rattlesnake is not beyond the realm of possibility for such a clever bird.

Why America's Rarest Bird Is So Rare

THE ivory-billed woodpecker, *Campephilus principalis,* America's rarest bird, now has a new lease on life. Thirteen hundred acres of Florida forest have been set aside to provide a sanctuary for the few ivorybills still left in the southern states.

Campephilus lives on the borers he digs from under the bark of trees which have died recently. And he needs lots of range. A pair of ivorybills, working together to feed a family, can strip the bark off all the dead trees in the neighborhood in a single nesting season. Then they must move on.

To keep eating, the ivorybill has to keep hacking away. If he runs out of dead trees, he meets with disaster— as he has already in deforested areas.

Will the ivory-billed woodpecker change his habits in his sanctuary? Will he find how to survive by feeding on other borers that can be found on living trees? No one knows, but the chances are that nature will find a way, now that campephilus has another chance.

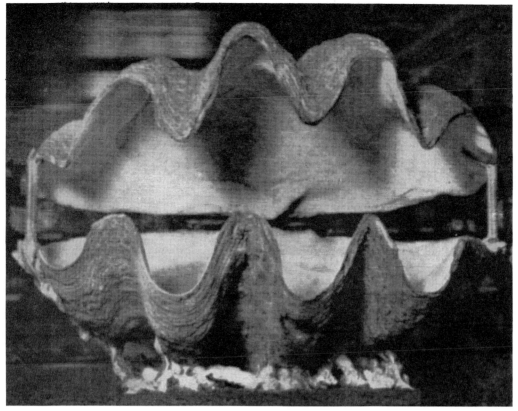

The "Man-Eating" Clam

ON the coral reefs off the jungle-clothed coasts of the Dutch East Indies, live the biggest clams in the world, *Tridacna gigantea.* Some of them reach a length of six feet and weigh nearly a ton.

"Man-eating clams" they have been called, but nothing could be further from the truth. Their food has to be almost microscopic, and so humans have no interest for them. However, though the clam does not prey upon men, it could kill a man. Gruesome stories are told by the natives of how men stepped in them unawares and had the great jaws close like a steel trap on their legs. If a man was caught in shallow water, unable to move, he could only watch the tide creep higher until he was drowned. If he was diving in deep water and was trapped, he could drown at once, remaining as food for the sharks.

Tridacna gigantea's pump system is its most important feature. In a closed membrane are two syphons. Through one, water is pumped into the interior of the cavity and bathes the gills. These aerate the blood, filter out the food particles, and send the water out through the other syphon.

Like other clams, it has fleshy insides encased in hard shell jaws which serve as protection. They're effective armor when closed, and if anything intrudes when they're open, they'll shut with a snap.

"Flying Tiger" in Quaker Gray

THE kingbird (*Tyrannus tyrannus*) isn't as large as a robin, and there's nothing regal about his appearance. His breast is white and his back is Quaker-gray.

It is not until the approach of a crow, or other enemy, that you see why the kingbird is called "king." Let a crow pass near its chosen territory, and the kingbird circles out at once like a fighter plane off to attack a bomber. He rises above the black intruder and darts at it savagely, swooping and diving with such determination and ferocity that the one desire of the crow is to escape. He will even swoop at an eagle, alighting on its back while he pecks and pulls at its neck and head feathers. This bird realizes that attack is the best defense, and that is one of the reasons for its survival.

The kingbirds feed mainly on insects and are entirely beneficial. Most farmers love them because they harry crows and hawks away from the chicken yards.

They nest from southern British Columbia and Nova Scotia to Texas and Florida, and winter from Mexico to northern South America.

Baby Puffinus is Bigger than his Parents

FOR a few weeks after they are born, the young of the shearwater, *Puffinus kuhlii borealis*, are crammed with food.

All day long their parents bring from the beach choice morsels for their fledglings. The young birds grow so fat from this forced feeding that, long before they leave the nest, they are bigger than their hard-working parents. The accumulated fat soon serves a good purpose. The grown-ups suddenly stop feeding their babies and fly away. Then the fledglings live off their fat until they're strong enough—and streamlined enough—to fly, so they can skim up their own food from the sea.

Nature's Gas Attack

NO American mammal is less popular than the skunk. It possesses a scent sac of malodorous fluid which it distributes with accuracy when annoyed. The odor is a most effective protection, for it is nauseating not only to man but to every wild enemy, the only exception being the great horned owl. Knowing that they are immune from attack, skunks saunter slowly through the woods or around farms and dwellings, never hurrying, always appearing to have unlimited leisure. The plumelike tail and the conspicuously striped body are warning signals which are seldom ignored. They are mostly nocturnal.

One of the marked characteristics of skunks is a fondness for the vicinity of man. They frequently take up quarters beneath out-buildings or under a house. Any convenient shelter appears to satisfy them, and they make their homes in deserted burrows of other animals, hollow logs, or in holes dug by themselves. A warm nest of grass and leaves is made at the end of the den, where the single litter of four to ten young is born in April or May. When the young are able to travel, they follow the mother, keeping behind her in a long line.

Skunks make delightful pets and play like kittens, seldom offering to bite or eject the evil-smelling fluid except under the greatest provocation.

The term "polecat" is sometimes used for all kinds of skunks, but the name is a misuse of that properly applied to the Old World martens.

The common skunk with its related species is found over almost all of the United States.

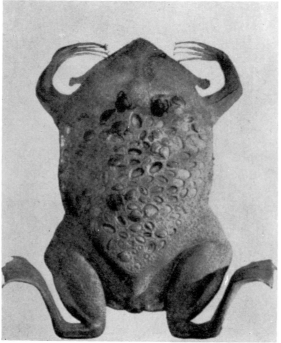

American Museum of Natural History

Pickaback Tadpoles

THE Surinam toad, *Pipa pipa,* of the Guianas and Brazil, takes no chances with its young. They're always with mother until they're full grown. In fact, mother keeps them *in* her back. As the eggs are laid the male distributes them over the back of the female and then presses the adhesive eggs into pits in her back. The female's back becomes soft as a featherbed and the delicate eggs sink into the epidermis where they are enveloped, each in a cup of soft skin with a lid on top. Here they grow, passing through the tadpole stage to maturity, when the young break through the lids and hop out.

[125]

They Make Their Own Swimming Pools

THE sound of tree frogs is inevitably associated with running brooks, budding trees, and unfolding flowers. Their cheerful songs are heard most often during damp weather and before a storm. Thus they have been given an undeserved reputation as weather prophets, but really it is only because they are stirred to life by unusual moisture in the air.

When a tree frog is not singing, he is a difficult little beast to find, for he can make himself resemble a bit of lichen or a green leaf by changing his body color to match the surroundings, but he cannot do it rapidly. It takes an hour to simulate a new spot that he finds comfortable. His best defense lies in his ability to keep perfectly still for hours on end.

All his fingers and toes are provided with adhesive tissues and a sticky substance by means of which he can climb with great skill.

The tree frogs hibernate when cold weather begins, and sleep continuously until the return of higher temperature. It may be for months or even years. And if warmth never returned, the sleep would continue until the little creature died from exhaustion of vital organs.

Most Hylas attach their many eggs to grass and leaves in shallow water, but *Hyla faber* can lay only a very few. She has overcome this disadvantage in a very ingenious way. Instead of laying her eggs where many of them would certainly be eaten by fish and insects—as other frogs do—she builds a strong corral of mud on the bank of the pond, and deposits her few precious eggs within this protective wall. There the tadpoles grow, quite safe from enemies, until they are strong and quick enough to take care of themselves in deep water.

The Beetle That Can Crash Dive

THE *Dineutes emarginata*, or whirligig beetle, is the shiny black insect most of us have seen skimming madly around on the surface of ponds. But, when necessary, he can give a pretty good imitation of a submarine going into a crash dive.

When danger appears, the whirligig beetle catches a bubble of air under his wing covers and quickly dives deep under the surface, where he can remain until the danger is past.

The Bird With the "Telescope Eyes"

VULTURES head the list of long-lived birds. In the Zoological Gardens at Giza, Egypt, a vulture lived for ninety-five years.

Vultures are repulsive birds except in flight, but they are health-protectors in warm lands where they eat carrion, being guided to their food not by smell—but by sight. Its amazing vision is an important factor in the vulture's longevity. Suddenly a vulture will appear from nowhere in the sky and drop directly downward to a dead animal no larger than a cat which it has seen although it was far beyond human vision. If one descends, it will be followed by others, until all the vultures for many miles around have congregated.

What the vulture lacks in beauty and grace on the ground, it gains in the air, where it is the embodiment of flying grace. Although its beak is powerful, its feet are weak and it never attempts to use them as does an eagle or a hawk.

Besides carrion, it eats snakes, toads, and probably rats and mice, but never attacks poultry or game birds.

The turkey vulture, or buzzard, is found in most of the southern states and as far north as British Columbia and northern Minnesota. The California condor and the black vulture of Asia are among the largest birds in the world, having a wing-spread of more than ten feet.

The Sour Butterfly

THE great brown Monarch butterfly, because it secretes an acid fluid which is distasteful to birds, is immune from their attacks. For this reason it is mimicked by other butterflies.

Most butterflies have only a few days of life, which centers about the spot where they were hatched, but others, like the Monarch, may travel thousands of miles before settling at last to lay their eggs. The Monarchs move southward singly or in enormous flocks. As many as a billion have been recorded in a single flight, requiring days to pass a given point, pressing on and on always southward. When they reach the Gulf States in November, the Monarchs settle in vast swarms on trees and bushes, there to sleep away the winter in a state of semihibernation. Often Monarchs use the same trees year after year in their Southland home, although the same individuals never return a second time. The great flocks break up in the spring and the Monarchs go northward, stopping to lay their eggs on the leaves of milkweed over almost all of North America from the Gulf States to Hudson Bay.

The larvae have greenish-white bodies banded with black and white, and bear on their backs two pair of slender filaments.

They have spread from North America to the Cape Verde Islands in the Atlantic, and to the islands of the Pacific, Australia and New Zealand.

[129]

The Bird With a Scoop-Shovel Mouth

IN his exploration of Louisiana's Feliciana wilderness in the 1820's, John James Audubon was often led to new bird-life discoveries by observations of the plantation Negroes.

It was from Pomp, one of these native naturalists, that Audubon first learned of the stealthy measures that the chuck-will's-widow took to keep her nest from being robbed by marauders. Touch the eggs of this shy bird, Pomp said, and the chuck-will's-widow would move them to a new nest.

Audubon had only to find a nest to prove that the chuck-will's-widow did move her eggs. But he had to spend a night in the brush beside a nest he had molested to discover how she moved them. Then, as the pine woods came to life with the dawn, he saw a pair of the birds fly from the nest, carrying the eggs in their beaks to another place for safekeeping.

The bird seeks its food near the ground, winging over the fields ready to snap up any flying insects. Nature has given it a veritable scoop-shovel mouth bordered with bristles. The tiny weak bill gives no indication of the enormous extent to which the mouth can be opened.

Chuck-will's-widows (*Antrostomus carolinensis*) breed from Missouri, Indiana, Ohio, and Virginia south to the Gulf States. During the day they lie concealed in secluded thickets or dark woods. Their plumage blends so marvelously with the foliage that they can be mistaken easily for a branch of leaves or a piece of bark. When dusk begins, they utter the monotonous cry from which their name is derived.

His Front Door Is a Waterfall

BIRDS find strange places for their nests, but the water ouzel, or dipper, has outdone them all in choosing a safe and romantic homesite. The female often builds her nest under, and behind, a waterfall.

Where a stream drops over a cliff, it pitches outward a short distance as it falls, leaving a mist-filled space between the waterfall and the rock. There, on some jutting ledge, the nest is placed.

This strange location has two distinct advantages for the dipper. Not only is the nest well hidden, but it has only one approach: through the falling water—and what animal would look for a bird's nest behind a curtain of spray? The birds have no difficulty in flying through the waterfall to the nest, for their dense plumage sheds water like a duck's.

The water ouzel is quite an ordinary-looking little fellow, but he has a certain spritelike quality that one never forgets. He lives near high, foaming Rocky Mountain streams, and has a strange habit of ducking into the water and walking unconcernedly on the bottom while he feeds upon aquatic insects and fish prey. He uses his wings as flippers.

The Lion Is a Gentleman

THE lion is a gentleman of the animal world. Slow to anger, knowing that he is supreme in strength, he stalks majestically across the African plains and will seldom attack unless wounded or provoked beyond reason. Moreover, he kills game only for food and not for the mere sport of killing as do some other carnivores.

The lion has a solid tawny color, so that while it is lying in undergrowth or among brown rocks or tall grass it is well concealed. This is not too important as far as protection is concerned, since the lion has no natural enemies, but it does enable it to kill its prey more easily. Zebras and antelopes are its favorite food. The lion will lie motionless in a thicket waiting until a herd of zebras feed near enough so that in a single quick dash it can land on the back of one.

Lions with long manes are seldom seen in the wild, for the thorns and bushes tear off the great mass of hair around their necks. Only in zoological gardens, or when a lion is in confinement, does the mane grow to a great length. The female has no mane.

Underwood & Underwood

The name "King of Beasts" is most aptly chosen. When one sees a lion walking with head up as though it owned the world, one realizes what a superb creature it is.

Many hundreds of years ago lions were found in Asia as well as in Africa, but they have all been exterminated in Asia except in one corner of northwestern India where a few individuals still remain under the rigid protection of an Indian prince.

The Bird That Didn't Know What To Do

WHEN the Portuguese landed on the island of Mauritius in the Indian Ocean during the sixteenth century, they found a strange, ungainly creature with disagreeable colorings. Although incapable of flight, it was a bird; somewhat larger than a turkey, it was related to the pigeon family.

This discovery was confirmed by later explorers, one of whom, an Emanuel Altham, wrote this note accompanying a specimen he sent back to Europe in 1628: "You shall receive—a strange fowle: which I had at the Iland Mauritius called by ye Portingalls a Do Do."

And, in 1638, Sir. T. Herbert wrote: "Here and no where else, that ever I could see or heare of, is generated the Dodo, a Portuguize name it is, and has reference to her simpleness."

But the dodo is no more. He exists only in a phrase, and there as the ultimate in oblivion: "as extinct as the dodo." It seems that around 1644 colonizers brought dogs and swine to the island. These thrived and multiplied and soon exterminated the dodo. This may not have been due so much to the fighting ability of the animals as to the docility of the dodo and the fact that it laid its solitary egg in a clump of grass on the ground where it could easily be trampled or devoured. The poor dodo could neither fight, flee, nor lay its eggs out of reach. It didn't know what to do to protect itself against the new dangers. The last report of a live dodo followed shortly.

The Caterpillar Who Pretends He's Been Eaten

THE caterpillar of the West African moth (*Nyctemera apicalis*) is an extraordinary artist when it comes to mimicry.

Like many of his cousins, he has dangerous parasitic enemies. It is the habit of these parasites to bore through the side of a cocoon and lay their eggs in the body of the caterpillar. When the caterpillar is full grown, the parasitic larvae devour him. Then they bore their way out of his cocoon and spin clusters of tiny, frothlike cocoons for themselves on the outside.

So the Nyctemera caterpillar goes to considerable trouble to prevent these enemies from breaking into his house.

When he spins his cocoon, he also produces from his body a series of frothy, cream-colored bubbles. As each is formed, he winds a few strands of silk around it, drags it off, and attaches it to the outside of his cocoon.

When his house is complete, the tiny bubbles clustered on it are an exact replica of cocoon clusters made by the invading parasite. Thus the caterpillar attempts to make his home secure by pretending that it has already been invaded.

Too Heavy To Handle

THE so-called "white rhinoceros" isn't white at all. The animal has a habit of wallowing in mud which dries on the skin, and at a distance it appears to be of a light gray color. The first explorers who saw the beast in the Congo region of Africa thought this was the natural color of the skin and called it the "white" rhinoceros, distinguishing it from the well-known black rhino. Naturalists know it as the square-lipped rhinoceros. It is the largest of the rhino group.

The two frontal "horns" are not true horns at all, but epidermal growths which are attached to the skin.

Like the black rhino, they are incredibly stupid beasts, but are irritable beyond reason. They have excellent hearing and a keen sense of smell, but the slightest disturbance is apt to send them charging about wildly; but their eyesight is so poor that once they lose the scent of an enemy, they stop in confusion and go lumbering off, puffing and grunting. Probably by that time they have forgotten what they started out to do.

The rhino has few enemies for, weighing two tons, he has the advantage of sheer weight; and also he has an enormously thick skin, which protects him from insects and other hazards against which weight does not matter. If man does not exterminate him, he'll probably continue to blunder his way through life for many centuries to come.

Barbed-Wire Plants

THE porcupine and the hedgehog are equipped with formidable quills. They form an armor that warns every enemy to let them severely alone or take the consequences, but their spines are nothing compared with those of some plants. The deadly cholla, or "jumping cactus," of the Arizona desert is clothed with incredibly sharp spines which detach themselves and fasten to one's flesh at the merest touch as do the porcupine's quills. The barrel cactus has terrible curved spines like fish hooks, and dozens of other species are so completely armored that one wonders how even birds ever find a resting place on their bristling stalks.

As a rule, nature has been less concerned about trees. Still, for some reason, she has taken particular care of the Central American acacia (*Acacia sphaerocephala*).

Its trunk and branches are covered with large, sharp thorns, set in pairs —from which it gets the name "Bull's-horn Thorn." These strong, curved spines, sticking out in every direction, warn you clearly to keep away.

But there's another reason for leaving the acacia severely alone.

Its formidable thorns are hollow. And living comfortably inside them you are likely to find numbers of stinging, biting ants, which swarm forth viciously at an intruder's touch and warn you to seek closer contact at your peril.

He Lives by His Wits

THE raccoon, by sheer intelligence, has held its own in much of its original range even though that country is thickly settled. He is so resourceful that he often prowls right into the suburbs of our largest cities. He is mischievous, full of fun, and seems to rely on his busy little brain to get him out of any difficulties.

When near water, he has a curious and unique habit of washing his food before eating it. An amusing experience is to give a captive raccoon a piece of lump sugar. He immediately runs to a basin of water to wash it as usual, but suddenly opens his hand to find that it has disappeared. He will return for another piece with the most amazed expression on his face. It requires only two or three failures, however, to make him realize that this particular food will not stand water.

Raccoons began to figure in our frontier literature at an early date. Coonskin caps, with the ringed tails hanging like plumes, made the favorite headgear of many pioneer hunters; and coonskins were a recognized article of barter at country stores.

Raccoons everywhere seek the wooded shores of streams and lakes. They are expert tree climbers, frequently having their dens in hollow trees. Although they are tree-frequenting animals, the greater part of their activities is confined to the ground, especially along water courses.

The hind feet rest flat on the ground, like those of a bear, and make tracks that have a curious resemblance to those of a very small child. The foretoes are long and separated, thus permitting the animal to use the front feet with almost the facility of a monkey's hands.

H. Armstrong Roberts

Actually Quicker than a Flash

A LOON can actually dive at the flash of a gun before the bullet reaches him. When he sees the flash, he gives a flip of his paddle-like feet and is safe beneath the water. He may emerge fifty or a hundred feet from where he went down, his head turning alertly in all directions. It is almost impossible to shoot a loon when he is looking at you. Nature has given him this extraordinary quickness as a means of protection—not principally from man, but from other enemies that find him good to eat.

He is a beautiful bird, about the size of a goose, with black and white barred feathers and a greenish iridescent head and neck.

The loon's legs are set further back on his body than those of other birds. This enables him to dive and swim better than many fish, but on land he is one of the most awkward creatures imaginable. He moves about like a lame man and is almost helpless.

To anyone who knows the northern wilderness, the loon brings visions of quiet lakes bordered by birch trees. His weird mournful cry is an inseparable part of our northern woodland lakes. The far-reaching wail comes across the water with a quality of unutterable melancholy. The weird call has given rise to the phrase "crazy as a loon," but the bird is far from crazy.

The female lays two eggs—usually in a substantial nest of grass and rushes, but always on a tiny island or very close to the shore.

When the young are hatched, they are ready to begin cruising soon after the sun has dried their brownish-black down. If the family is approached, the young dive and make short trips under water. Meantime, the parents flop about as though they were crippled and make frantic efforts to lure the intruder away from the track taken by their young.

Late in August or September, the old ones pass much time upon the wing, circling about the lake encouraging the young to acquire strength in flight, for during migration southward, the babies will be led out to sea where they will have to shift for themselves.

The common loon (*Gavia immer*) breeds from Labrador and Nova Scotia south to northern New York and in Iceland. It spends its winter from the Great Lakes to the Gulf Coast, and the eastern side of the Atlantic to the Mediterranean and Black Sea.

The Streamlined Mackerel

THE *Scomber scombrus*, the common mackerel which roams the seas of the North Atlantic, is the perfect embodiment of streamlining.

His slim, iridescent body is long and spindle-shaped, designed especially for great endurance. He has strong muscles along his spinal column and can tuck his fins in close to his body so as to swim with a minimum of effort.

Nature has equipped the mackerel in this fashion because he has a serious handicap. Unlike most fish, he has no air bladder to give him buoyancy.

[141]

If he happened to be in shallow water, he could sink to rest on the bottom without being endangered by the pressure of water above him. But as he spends much of his life far out in the open sea, this solution is usually impossible.

He cannot suspend himself motionless near the surface like those fish with air bladders. Yet, if he should allow himself to sink, the pressure of the depths would crush him. So, as long as he is in the open sea, he can never rest, but must keep swimming constantly to avoid disaster.

The Fish That Can Live on Land

ONE of the most remarkable creatures in the world is the lungfish (*Protopterus*) which looks like an eel and lives much like any other fish except that it must rise to the surface to breathe. But during the annual dry season of the tropics, it demonstrates its extraordinary abilities. If it is trapped in a swamp by the recession of water, it burrows into the ground. It covers itself with a cocoon of dried slime, secreted by its skin glands, which completely envelops the body except at the mouth. This prevents the moisture in the body from drying out completely. As the water disappears, the fish rolls itself in a tight coil and goes to sleep. In the hard mud the creature is as effectively imprisoned as though it were buried in cement, yet it can live there for from one to five years.

It can exist without food for a long while by living on its own fat and body tissues, and it has lungs as well as gills. Its life span is more than one hundred years.

The lungfish is literally a "living fossil"—the survivor of an incredibly ancient group once common in the fresh waters of the Paleozoic continents two hundred million years ago. It is an example of "arrested development." Some time long ago, when the waters of the earth were receding, it started to change from an aquatic creature to a land creature. But having found a way to exist despite the absence of water, it stopped changing and persisted as it was—an in-between creature living in the water when there was water, hibernating in the mud when necessary.

Now there are only three **representatives** of the group—one each in Australia, South America, Africa.

A number of encrusted lungfish have been dug out and shipped to various parts of the world in their blocks of mud. Some of these were wakened by immersion in water and kept in aquaria for years. When the mud nests were opened, the lungfish were in a state of profoundest sleep. They could be handled or kept for weeks without awakening; their sleep was like that of a very tired child, quite indifferent to the outside world, until they were put in water when they woke up immediately.

New York Zoological Society

He Has a Built-In Loud-Speaker

THE kangaroo rat (*Dipodomys spectabilis*) lives in an underground house in the dry, burning sand wastes of the western deserts. But lack of water doesn't bother him, for, like some other rodents, he gets enough liquid for his bodily needs by converting the starch in his food into water, and all his life he never touches a drop of fluid.

Despite his name, Dipodomys is neither a kangaroo nor a rat, but is a near relative of the pocket mouse which shares his desert haunts. His dwelling is a maze of tunnels and cozy chambers, with many exits, any of which Dipodomys can reach in a flash should a coyote, or other enemy, start digging for him. Even such a silent intruder as a snake, slithering down one of his front halls, seldom catches Dipodomys unawares, for he hears two ways— through the air and through the ground. Large resonance chambers, which take up half of his skull space, allow him to detect dangerous visitors through the ground vibrations they make as well as the sounds.

Dipodomys has no vocal call note, but he makes a low drumming sound when in the burrow by beating the soles of his hind feet on the ground, producing a tiny vibrating roar. This may be an alarm signal, a call note, or a challenge to other males. He has another method of communication, too, for on his back between the shoulders is a large unctuous gland that secretes a waxy matter of peculiar smell. Whenever the gland touches a rock or bush, it leaves an odor, and lets his friends know that he has passed that way.

[144]

The Crab Who Uses Hand Grenades

CRAB of the Indian Ocean (*Melia tessellata*) has feeble claws, ill-suited for defense. He isn't a particularly large crab either, nor does he have an extremely hard shell. And his enemies are many.

Hordes of hungry fish hunt food in the coral reefs where this crab makes his home. These undersea raiders have strong teeth, and they like crab-meat.

But those who seek to make a meal of *Melia tessellata* discover to their pain that he travels armed. In each of his feeble claws he carries something that serves as a hand grenade. It is a sea anemone and it can deliver a very painful sting.

When the crab is going to be attacked, these living weapons warn the foe away. Then, if the warning is ignored, the aggressor feels the stinging tentacles of the anemones.

So *Melia tessellata* is left pretty much alone, and thrives amidst many dangers. The stinging anemones give him the protection his own physical make-up lacks.

A Porcupine Can't Shoot His Quills

IKE the skunk, who knows that no animal can tolerate his nauseating odor, the porcupine ambles slowly through the northern forests of the United States and Canada, serenely confident that he is impervious to attack.

His armor is a special development of the fur into rigid, sharp-pointed spines, or quills, two or three inches in length. The spines usually lie flat on the body, but when the animal is excited or alarmed, they may be raised by special muscles on the under side of the skin into a bristling array of barbed points. The quills are so slightly attached that when their tips enter the skin of an animal they at once become free at the base. If not extracted, they gradually work deeper into the flesh by muscular action, and may eventually cause death.

When annoyed, the porcupine arches his back, and, with his spines bristling in every direction, calmly awaits the enemy. The instant he is touched, the animal whips his armed tail about, and the attacker is pierced by a host of stinging darts. This swift and effective flip of the tail has given rise to the popular fallacy that the porcupine can "shoot" its quills to some distance.

Porcupines have an intimate connection with the romantic side of early Indian life in America. Their white quills were colored in bright hues by vegetable dyes known to the Indians, and served to make embroidery on moccasins and other articles of clothing.

The Raccoon That Looks Like a Bear

THE amusing and amusing-looking panda that has captured the popular fancy is really the GIANT PANDA, *Ailuropoda melanoleuca*. He has been known to science less than one hundred years, and it was less than fifteen years ago that the first panda was seen outside of Asia.

Probably that was because the panda's habitat was so hidden from the rest of the world. He comes from deepest Asia, high up in the remote mountains of Szechwan and Kansu. In addition to that he is further protected by the fact that he lives in the secure fastnesses of the bamboo jungles. He feeds almost entirely on bamboo shoots which are right at hand in plentiful supply. Because of his strong teeth he has no trouble in chewing the bamboo, and has this food almost to himself. There's no reason for him to roam far away from his bamboo home. He has a pretty easy life and so is charmingly playful. He likes to clown around and is a delightful companion. But adult pandas have long claws, useful to them in the jungle, but harmful to humans. Baby giant pandas are fine as pets, adults are not.

Scientists couldn't at first decide whether pandas were bears or raccoons. They looked like bears, but as their skulls and other parts were examined it was decided they belonged to the raccoon family in a subfamily called the *Ailurinae*.

"He Hung on Like an Ant"

H E hung on like a bulldog is a common phrase, but, if one really wants to express tenacity, one ought to say, "He hung on like an ant." One observer, who watched a dead grasshopper being dragged along by an ant, weighed the bodies of both. He found that the ant was pulling a load sixty times its own weight. This is equivalent to a man whose weight is one hundred and fifty pounds dragging a load four and a half tons, or a horse weighing twelve hundred pounds pulling a load of thirty-six tons. An Australian ant, while suspending itself by its feet, supported a pair of gloves which were more than eleven hundred times its own weight. To equal this, a one-hundred-and-fifty-pound man would have to support in his teeth a weight of eighty-two and a half tons while hanging by his toes.

Once fighting ants get a good hold, they never let go. Mutilation or death fails to loosen their grip. Even when their heads are cut off, their jaws will remain clamped to the bodies of their adversaries. It is reported that in India and Algeria ants are used by natives in surgery where we would employ adhesive plaster or stitches. The edges of a wound are pressed together with the left hand and an ant held in the right hand. The jaws of the ant are widely opened, and as the insect is gradually brought near the wound, it seizes both edges, holding them together. Then the "surgeon" snips off the bodies and the heads remain until the wound is healed.

Yes, it would be better to say, "He hung on like an ant."

The Co-operative Bee

*A*LTHOUGH the common honeybee (*Apis mellifera*) is not physically equipped to withstand cold weather, she is often found in climates where winters are severe.

And, unlike some insects whose life span is no longer than a season, a honeybee may live through the winter and into the following spring.

This is possible only because of the ingenious co-operative system by which she manages to keep warm, even at low temperatures.

The bees ball together in the hive, those in the center generating heat by moving constantly in a sort of dance. At intervals, they change places. Those that have been outside, exposed to the cold, go to the center.

By pooling resources in this way, honeybees are able to protect themselves from serious danger which they could not meet singly.

L. W. Brownell

The Little Miner

DR. E. W. NELSON says: "The mole is an expertly constructed living mechanism for tunneling through the earth. A pointed nose, short neck, compactly and powerfully built, ribs strongly braced to withstand pressure, and short paddlelike hands armed with strong claws for digging are all fitted for a single purpose. Eyes and ears are of little service in his ground life, so they have become practically obsolete. The fur has been modified to a thick, velvety coat which will lie either front or back with equal facility and thus relieve any friction from the walls of the tunnel roads no matter which way the animal travels. . . .

"Where the soil is loose, the mole practically swims through it, urged forward by powerful strokes of its hands and feet. This is the common mode of travel near the top of the ground where the course is marked by the upheaved and slightly broken surface. When working at a greater depth and in more compact soil, the mole must dig its way and dispose of the loose earth by pushing it along the tunnel to an outlet at the surface through which it is thrust to form a mound."

Moles are most abundant in open grassy areas, especially in meadows where the dense, rich soil affords a plentiful supply of earthworms, grubs, and insects upon which they feed.

Like a human miner, they lead a life of great activity and almost constant hard labor.

They have a habit of coming to the surface regularly to hunt food during the night when earthworms swarm about. At such times many are captured by owls, cats, and other beasts of prey.

Moles are circumpolar in distribution, being found from England to Japan in the Old World, and on both the Atlantic and Pacific Coasts, the only places they appear in North America.

Wild and Woolly Pig

THERE are only two species of wild swine in America. The collared peccary, *Pecari angulatus*, is the more common variety and it is found from Arkansas and Texas all the way down through South America. He has a razorbacked body but he is not the well-known half-wild razorback hog of the American Southwest. The collared peccary is really wild and really tough, roams in packs of a dozen or more and does not hesitate to attack humans. His weapons consist of short and flat but murderously sharp tusks and a "gas attack" gland on his back which can emit a disagreeable odor. The peccary's body is covered with long, wiry, oily hair, with a grayish white stripe, forming a sort of a collar, around his neck. The white-lipped peccary is the one other wild swine in America, but that species appears only from Central America south.

[151]

The Tree That Blinds

FROM time immemorial the manchineel tree has brought injury and, according to legend, death to natives of islands in the Caribbean.

Early histories of these places contain forbidding descriptions of its malignant powers. "So dire is the Manchineel that the very sun, darting its rays upon it, calls forth its dangerous odours and renders it unsafe to the touch. . . . The apples, if eaten, are said to be certain death to anything but goats."

Much of this is pure fantasy, but the fact remains that juices of the tree cause severe inflammation and acute conjunctivitis, if they come in contact with skin or eyes.

An early authentic account of the tree was furnished by Mr. Seemann, of His Majesty's good ship *Herald,* who wrote his report around 1850. Carpenters of his ship were rendered blind merely by cutting down one of the trees for lumber.

When he investigated the case, his eyes, too, were affected, although he only gathered some of the tree's leaves and bright-colored, sweet-smelling apples.

Happily, all regained sight, but from then on they eyed the manchineel from a safe distance.

His Home Is His Castle

ALTHOUGH their white coats make Rocky Mountain "goats" conspicuous as they climb around rocky ledges amid a wilderness of glacier-carved escarpments, they have few natural enemies due to the forbidding character of their haunts. The golden and bald eagles now and then kill the kids, but the lynx and mountain lion are not known to prey upon them to any considerable extent.

They are marvelously sure-footed and fearless in traversing the faces of high precipitous slopes, jumping from one ledge to another where it would seem that an animal even half their size could not move in safety.

Through summer and winter, goats find sufficient food in the scanty vegetation growing among the rocks, and their thick hair protects them from the fiercest winter blizzards.

In America the Rocky Mountain goat is the only representative of the goat-antelope group which centers in Asia. They range from Alaska east and south through the mountains of Montana and Washington.

The Bird Who Lives on a Raft

"HELL diver," "water witch," "didapper" are local names for the same bird. Scientifically it is known as the pied-billed grebe (*Podilymbus podiceps*), and it lives in ponds and lakes all over America. At a distance one could easily mistake the grebe for a duck, but the thin chickenlike bill with its dark stripe is far from ducklike. Watch one for a few moments and you will realize that the name "water witch" is well chosen. She can dive at the flash of a gun and be under the surface before the shot reaches where she was.

She is an expert swimmer and can lower her body in the water to any degree, both while swimming and remaining still. Often, when danger is near, she sinks until only her bill and eyes show above the surface. Safe in this position, she can remain until the baffled hunter or hawk goes on his way.

But the most remarkable thing about the grebe is her choice of a home. For, unlike most water birds that build their nests in the sand or rocks on shore, she builds on the water.

From buoyant stems of water plants she makes a small, floating platform with a slight depression in the middle for her eggs. This raft is generally attached to living reeds so it can float up and down but not move away.

When the grebe leaves her nest, she covers up the eggs, and her home is safely disguised as a small mass of floating green. Thus the home is well adapted both to her convenience and her ability to protect it.

The Crab That Condemns Itself to Prison

IN the Great Barrier Reef, off Australia, grow colonies of corals among which lives *Hapalocarcinus marsupialis*, a species of tiny crab.

In securing protection against her enemies, the female crab of this species, while still young, condemns herself to prison for life.

She takes up her home in the fork of two coral branches, and by constant movement sets up a current which seems to influence the coral's growth in a peculiar way. The branches broaden, curve out, then curve in again and unite over the crab's head, thus forming a round cage about the size of a marble.

Small holes let the sea flow in and out, bringing the tiny particles on which the crab feeds.

And there—snug, safe, protected from the hazards of her undersea world, but unable ever to venture out into that world again—she lives for the rest of her life.

Insect Impostors

WE have mentioned before that insects are the greatest mimics and we have shown a few examples like amphidasis and the walking stick. There are countless other pretenders that exist by imposture, by making themselves look like something dangerous or something useless. Here we show a few varied types.

Those are not thorns you see on the left but tree hoppers (*Umbonia crassicornis*), sometimes called Insect Brownies. The tree hopper has a sort of thorn projecting from its hard back and almost all birds are fooled into overlooking the tree hoppers, hiding in the open, on a tree trunk. *Umbonia crassicornis* is found in Central and South America.

[156]

Black Star

That's not a dried-up bunch of leaves below but an insect called *Extasoma tiaratum*. It's a distant cousin of the walking stick, one of the phasmatidae from Australia and New Guinea.

In South Africa there's a long-horned grasshopper, *Cycloptera camillifolia*, that escapes the depredations of birds and reptiles by managing to look like a tobacco leaf, uninteresting as food to the grasshopper's enemies. You can easily spot his picture here, but you'd probably never be able to spot him alive on a South African tree.

You certainly wouldn't try to catch that bee down below. He looks like a mean one, and if you disturbed him he'd buzz like a saw and wind up to sting you. But you needn't be afraid. He's a faker, he isn't a bee at all though he acts like one and his shape, size and coloration are those of a honeybee. He's a Drone Fly and quite harmless. Others that use the same trick are the Bumblebee Hawk Moth and the Soldier Fly.

Black Star

A Bird That Never Sees What It Eats

THE woodcock (*Philohela minor*) feeds by driving her three-inch bill into the mud. The highly sensitive tip feels earthworms upon which she feeds, and she never sees what she eats. With her face pressed close to the ground while she is feeding, she would be blind to the approach of enemies were it not that nature has given her protection. Her eyes have migrated up and back so that they are almost in the top of her head and she can see to either side and backward better than straight ahead.

Her nest is merely a depression in the leaves on the ground. Yet her coloring is so finely blended with her surroundings that enemies can pass close by and never know she is there. Her camouflage is so effective that she seldom finds it necessary to fly up from her nest at the approach of danger.

There is a popular misconception that during the nesting season, if she thinks her young are in danger, she will sometimes rise swiftly into the air with a chick grasped between her feet, and fly with it to safety. Then, if she still has the opportunity, she will return and carry off the remaining chicks one by one till all are safe. This is an example of nature folklore like the hoop-snake which is supposed to take its tail in its mouth and roll downhill and like the bridge of monkeys across a stream. How these false notions start no one knows, but they continue generation after generation although they have no foundation in fact.

He Wears His Own Backdoor

CHLAMYPHORUS TRUNCATUS has a name almost as long as himself, for his total length is only five or six inches. But he has the distinction of being smallest of the armadillos, and he is armed in a unique way.

The whole upper surface is covered by an armor shield which sits loosely on his body, fastened along the back by means of a loose membrane. The armor gapes open along the sides of the body and can be raised in a flaplike manner.

His front end comes to a rather sharp point. But, from the rear, he looks as though he had met with a buzz saw. And his square-cut tail end is covered with a bony shield, hard and glasslike.

While his sawed-off torso adds little to Chlamyphorus' beauty, it does help him to keep out of the way of trouble. When he meets a snake or other enemy, Chlamyphorus turns tail, scoots for his burrow, and digs himself in.

With his powerful, spadelike paws he wedges his body tightly into the ground. Then his rear-end shield becomes a strong, securely sealed back door, closing the burrow perfectly and protecting him from harm.

He lives in South America in the Argentine and is so rare that very little is known about his habits except that he is a lover of sandy plains, digs long tunnels under ground, and burrows with great speed because of his long claws which are useful as digging spades.

The Sea Wolves

THE killer "whale" is not really a whale, but the largest of the porpoise family. It is terrible in strength and ferocity. Afraid of neither man nor beast, it will attack anything that swims although it is only twenty-five or thirty feet long. The mighty teeth in its jaws can tear even a giant whale to bits. Its capacity is almost unbelievable. There is a record of thirteen porpoises and fourteen seals having been taken from the stomach of a twenty-one-foot killer. Killer whales, like wolves, attack in packs.

Killers attack whales several times their own length and eat out the tongue. The California gray whale is one of their chief victims. Even though they are fifty feet long, the big gray whales are in such terror of the sea wolves that when a pack arrives, they become absolutely paralyzed with fright. At times they will turn on their backs, with flippers outstretched, and lie helpless at the surface. Rushing at full speed, a killer will put his nose against a whale's lips, force its mouth open, and gouge out great chunks of the soft, sponge-like tongue. In the meantime other killers are tearing at the giant body, literally eating the whale alive. Killers would certainly attack men in the water, and they are not afraid of boats or even small ships.

Killers are found in all oceans of the world and dominate the seas in which they live.

The Collapsible Toad Who Submerges on Land

A STRANGE, weird-looking creature is the hermit spade-foot when you turn him out of his ground burrow. At first sight he seems to be a small, brown ball of earth but almost immediately air is expelled from the lungs so that his sides collapse. Two elevations rise from the smaller end and become staring eyes of such a brilliant gold color that they seem wholly out of place in such a dusky surrounding. Awkward hands are lifted one at a time and rubbed over the eyes.

The spade-foot, now quite awake and alert, tries to escape. He has a unique way of protecting himself. He does not creep away stealthily, as do many of the toads, or startle you with a prodigious leap; instead, he begins sinking out of sight in the soft earth and, in less time than it takes to tell, he has wholly disappeared from view. If the earth is removed carefully from over him, we find him cozily settled in his usual hibernating position. His head is bent downward so that his chin rests on his front feet, his legs are tucked closely under him, his eyes are shut, and his sides are pushed out because of the expansion of the lungs within. If he is taken out and put on some solid substance, and finds that digging efforts are unavailing, he creeps stealthily forward or hops in regular toad fashion for a short distance and then tries again to dig a burrow in which to hide.

The hermit spade-foot is not well known. It burrows into the ground and sleeps days or weeks, perhaps years, at a time. The mystery surrounding the life of a spade-foot is increased by the fact that he is wholly nocturnal in habit.

The only time when the spade-foot toads make themselves conspicuous is when they come out of their burrows hundreds strong and go to the ponds for the purpose of depositing their eggs. After the eggs are laid, the toads disappear entirely, leaving no trace of their hiding places. Not even a stray one is left behind and they may not appear again in the same locality for many years.

The hermit spade-foot is found in every part of eastern North America, including Texas and Florida.

The Bird That Looks Like a Snake

ANYONE who has been in the swamps of Florida must have seen the strange water turkey, or snakebird (*Anhinga anhinga*), for he lives along the sluggish bayous and rivers of the Gulf Coast and other parts of the subtropical bogs of America north to North Carolina. He is an extraordinary-looking bird with a slender snakelike neck and a long tail.

Although he spends much of his time in the water and feeds entirely upon fish, for some reason he does not have water-repellent feathers as do ducks and geese. His feathers are more like fur and soon become thoroughly soaked, so during the day he sits with his companions in a dead tree with wings half spread, drying his feathers in the sun.

He knows he is very conspicuous and so makes no attempt at concealment, but depends upon his wonderful eyesight and another method of
protection. If danger threatens, he drops like an arrow into the water; and
when he reappears, only the slender snakelike neck shows above the surface. Sometimes he will stiffen his sinuous neck, slowly ease his head out of
the water sticking it straight up, and remain absolutely motionless. To his
most discerning foes, the snakebird then seems exactly like a dead limb protruding from the mud.

Even Oysters Have Thorns

ONE of the many strange and colorful creatures who inhabit the corals
of tropic seas is the thorny oyster (*Spondylus pictorum*).

Like most mollusks, the thorny oyster starts early in life to build a hard
shell-fortress which he keeps enlarging as he grows. This protects his soft,
defenseless body from many misfortunes.

But he is surrounded by dangers from which the hardness of his shell,
alone, could not defend him.

Large fish with teeth that can easily crush a mollusk shell are always
swimming among the corals in search of food. And, unlike the deep-sea
scallop, the thorny oyster cannot skip about to elude these potential enemies. He is usually attached to a coral by one of his valves.

So nature has provided a special defense for his fortress in order to make it doubly secure. In contrast to the ordinary oyster shell, his shell bristles with long spines which curve outward in a menacing fashion. With these formidable weapons, the thorny oyster keeps danger at a safe distance.

The Good-Natured Rat

MUCH the largest of the gnawing animals is an aquatic rodent called the capybara. It's about the size of a pig (four feet long, weighing about 100 pounds), lives on the shores of streams and rivers and dives into the water when frightened. He has strong webbed feet and can swim under water for amazingly long distances but he's rather clumsy at walking and running. Capybara is a vegetarian and is likely to do damage to sugar cane or other crops but he's not vicious. In fact, he's easily tamed, loves to play and is extremely good-natured. On the other hand, he is considered to be very stupid. Capybara, *Hydrochoerus hydrochoerus,* comes from tropical America.

He Can Walk on the Ceiling

THE Egyptian gecko, *Tarentola annularis,* has an armory of tricks and defenses. Most notable is its equipment of adhesive digits so constructed that it can climb up the side of a room, walk upside-down on a ceiling, hang on the lower side of large leaves. Also a gecko can discard his tail at will, leaving the tail writhing and twisting in a manner likely to direct the enemy's attention while the gecko himself makes good his escape. In effect, this is like the old legend of "throwing something to the wolves." And if the gecko does get away by means of this ruse, he'll simply grow a new tail.

Geckos are lizards, have large eyes with vertical elliptical pupils, are not only harmless to humans but rather are useful to man because they destroy insects. Their cry sounds like "gecko," and that accounts for the name.

Build a House to Catch a Wife

TROGLODYTES is the British representative of the wren family which is widely distributed in the northern hemisphere.

The male wren has an unusual way of getting a wife. He establishes himself in a territory, claiming possession with a song of surprising vigor for so small a bird, and then starts to work on two or three nests using mostly leaves and lichens for the walls. At last he succeeds in attracting a female, who looks over the houses he has prepared, examines him with a view to matrimony, and if she is pleased with him and the fruits of his labor, she proceeds to select one of his sample homes and to furnish it.

When the nesting spot is an ancient, moss-grown tree trunk, Troglodytes shapes his nest to look like a decaying knot. The bird makes a door in the side to further the illusion, and sheathes the nest with the same moss that covers the tree.

Against a haystack, Troglodytes builds a nest with a covering of loose hay. And in a cranny in a lichen-covered wall, his home is camouflaged with lichens. To conceal the nest and keep the fledglings from harm, Troglodytes adapts the building plans to suit the nesting site.

In the winter, a well-built nest is utilized as a dormitory. Sometimes as many as fourteen wrens will huddle together in the old nest.

His Wings Are His Padlock

THE bark beetle (*Pityogenes hopkinsi*) is a brown and black midget less than one twelfth of an inch long. But, for his size, he is amazingly strong. His jaws are so powerful that he can eat the bark and wood of the white pine where he spends his life.

To make his home, he tunnels right through the bark and hollows out a tiny chamber in the wood beneath. From here the female beetles make egg galleries and raise their families.

But perhaps the most interesting thing about this little beetle is the way the male zealously protects his young. After his home is built, he "locks" the door. Firmly wedging the back ends of his wings into the entrance of the tunnel, he maintains his position so tenaciously, that it is almost impossible for any enemy to dislodge him and push past.

The Kangaroo Needs No Baby Sitters

WHEN the young of some kangaroos are born, they are no larger than an aspirin tablet. The mother transfers them immediately to the abdominal pouch where they nurse continually. Even after the babies are large enough to run, when danger threatens, they scamper back to the mother and climb into her pouch. Thus the pouch not only provides safety

for the young, but it also enables the kangaroo to attend to the main business of living without the normal bother of baby care.

Kangaroos have exceedingly long and strong hind legs but the forelimbs are small and used only for grasping. The animal runs by a series of immense bounds with the foreparts of the body held forward and balanced by the great tail. When not moving, kangaroos stand upright, the tail and hind limbs acting as a tripod. This position enables them to use sight, smell, and hearing to detect enemies.

The hind foot has a very long toe with a curved and pointed claw. This is a dangerous weapon. A large kangaroo can kill a dog by grasping it with his forepaws and inflicting terrible wounds with the saberlike hind claw.

Paternalism in the Nest

IF you have ever watched a nest of young yellow warblers carefully, you have observed that both parents co-operate in the job of feeding the babies. Sometimes the mother sits on the nest while the father forages for worms, seeds, and other delicacies. Sometimes both the mother and father hunt for food.

But the mother is never left alone to shoulder the complete care of her young if there are more than two young birds in the nest. Perhaps without the care and attention of both parents the yellow warbler might be exterminated.

Because its nest is easily found, this bird is often victimized by the infamous cowbird. However, this is one of the few birds—and perhaps the only species—which resents and often defeats the cowbird's attempt to unload its parental responsibility. Sometimes the clever warbler builds a platform over the alien egg and continues her domestic affairs as originally planned. Indeed, two cowbird eggs have been found in a nest, each covered up by a separate layer of nest material.

The yellow warbler is sometimes called the wild canary. It is one of the commonest of the warbler tribe, and ranges over a vast extent of territory, being found from ocean to ocean.

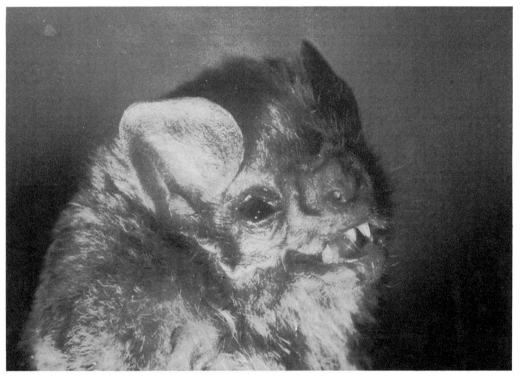

Charles E. Mohr, The National Audubon Society

The Vampire's Secret Weapon

IN European mythology, the vampire was supposed to be the soul of a corpse which left the grave at night to suck the blood of sleeping persons. It was said to assume the shape of werewolves, birds, snakes, or even cats and dogs but *bats* were never mentioned.

When Cortez followers returned from Central America in the early sixteenth century, however, they brought an actual basis for their superstition. They had encountered a bat which really lived on the blood of animals and humans alike. From that story all bats became blood-suckers in their legends, although we know now that the only blood-drinking bats in the world inhabit the American tropics. They all belong to the family *Desmodontidae*.

A number of zoologists have carried on most interesting experiments both in the field and laboratory to discover whether or not the vampire actually does suck blood and if so, how he does it. They found that the bat doesn't *suck* blood, but that he *drinks* it. He alights gently on his victim and walks about with his body well elevated until he finds a spot to his liking. Then, with his sharp curved teeth, he makes a small incision so painlessly that his victim hardly feels it. As the blood flows, he laps it up with his tongue but never sucks it. The vampire's saliva contains an ingredient which prevents the blood from coagulating, thus insuring a free flow. The bats particularly attack the delicate flesh under the surfaces of one's toes.

A. C. Ruthven, writing of an expedition to Colombia, says that his men discovered one night that they had been raided by vampire bats and the

Charles E. Mohr, The National Audubon Society

whole party was covered with blood stains from the many bites of these little animals. They were not disturbed in their sleep, for there was no pain at the time of the bite, nor indeed, for some hours afterward. If the vampires' bites had been painful, if it were necessary for them to keep on biting in order to keep the blood flowing, they would have been scared away or caught. But they had found a way, secret and painless, to feed safely and well.

Milk Cows for Ants

DR. WILLIAM MANN first observed the strange family life of the curious ant, *Polyrhachis simplex,* when he explored the Kerak region of Palestine in 1914.

Small silk-and-leaf structures that the explorer found on bushes near his tent were the tip-off that Polyrhachis was living in the vicinity. Each of these structures sheltered leaf hoppers, which exuded a kind of nectar that the ants fed on. The ants were sheltering the hoppers, as humans keep milk cows, to furnish food for the colony.

But it was not until he located the ant nest and followed the trails leading from it that Dr. Mann discovered how the aerial cow barns for the food-producing leaf hoppers were built.

Worker ants were carrying Polyrhachis' newly hatched larvae to the building site. Then, these infants set to work spinning the silk to make shelters for the family's milk cows.

A. DURENCEAU

This Desert Rat Has Snowshoes

THE African jerboa is unusually equipped. He is protected by several extraordinary features. Jerboa, *Jaculus jaculus*, is a rat who lives on the desert.

Though he's only five inches high, he can jump fifteen feet in one hop, using his very long tail as a balancing rudder. That long tail with its pad at the end also helps form a tripod, permitting jerboa to stand erect.

He has 360-degree vision. He can see ahead, behind, above or below—all around—without turning his neck.

His hind feet are heavily haired and act like snowshoes so that jerboa doesn't sink into the loose sand but rather skims quickly over it, erect and looking just like a running bird.

He Lives in an Armored Castle

SOME animals grow protective armor on their own bodies, but the hermit crab does things much more simply. He crawls into the unoccupied shell of a mollusk and carries this impenetrable house about with him whenever he moves.

Because of its habit of living in a hard domicile, the body has become greatly changed. Its abdomen within the mollusk shell is long, slender, and soft, and the large claws effectively block the opening to the shell. A pair of hooklike abdominal appendages near the end of the abdomen allow the animal to cling securely to ridges in his adopted home.

Whenever the crab grows too big for its house, it lets go with its abdominal hooks, crawls out and into a new and larger shell. Sometimes the shells are the base for corals, barnacles, sponges, and other sea life, which do the crab no harm and enjoy the benefits of a wandering life.

Hermit crabs feed on fresh or old meat and have the unattractive habit of cannibalism. They are great fighters, and as a penalty for defeat, the vanquished crab provides a meal for the victor.

Lightning Change Artist

IMAGINE a lizard with a prehensile tail, the mechanical turrets of a tank to act as eyes, a tongue which can shoot out and capture an insect more than a body's length away, and a skin which can change color to resemble the branch upon which it is sitting—and you have the incredible chameleon.

Many lizards have tails that are so inconsequential they can be lost at a moment's notice and be regrown at leisure, but the chameleon's tail is a delicate organ with nerves and a fine sense of feeling. It constantly wraps itself around twigs to prevent a fall.

Mr. Lewis Walker says: "The chameleon's use of its legs, body, and prehensile tail is deliberate and drawn-out either when it is releasing one branch or grasping a new one. But this lethargic demeanor stops with the eyes as they rotate in their turret sockets. These unique organs project prominently from the sides of the head as cone-shaped turrets capable of revolving in any direction. The eyes rotate at the outermost points of the cones, making it possible for a chameleon to see his nose, forehead, and perhaps even his opposite eye without undue strain. While one eye scans the ground below for possible enemies, the other is searching the branches above for insects; but they work in unison when prey is sighted. This can be a fly, beetle, or worm, and as far as ten inches away from a six-inch lizard. When the range is right, the two eyes again swing to the front, and the mouth of the lizard opens. Suddenly the insect disappears from the branch and dangles on the sticky edge of a stringlike tongue. The out-thrust is lightninglike, but the return is slower and can be watched. The tongue contracts like a rubber band and thickens with the bug still held captive on the end. . . .

"The word 'chameleon' is almost synonymous with changing color. However, the color is not necessarily governed by background, for many of the changes are emotional and just as difficult to control as a human's blush."

Two dozen young are born in thin membranes, and on emergence are wet and sticky. The babies sedately climb to the higher branches of a tree where they appear to mimic their mother, with their tiny tails wrapped around twigs.

A Dog's Worst Friend

HUNTING dogs have the greatest respect for the badger, whose curious squat form seems designed as a counter-offensive against dogs. It has a low flattened body and short thick legs, so that a dog finds it hard to get at him. Also, it has long claws on its forefeet, useful in fighting as well as in digging. And to top it all, the badger has very strong jaws and

New York Zoological Society

good long teeth. He's a tough, persistent fighter, noted for his indomitable courage. Nevertheless, it is the badger's unusual low center of gravity that is its basic protection.

The scientific name of the badger is *Taxidea taxus*, and he is found all over the temperate areas of the United States and Canada, Europe and Asia. Its popular name is said to derive from the peculiar white badge on its head.

The Great Sleeper

THE woodchuck is a typical marmot with coarse hair, heavy body, short neck, powerful legs, and feet armed with strong claws for digging. He is a well-known inhabitant of fields and grassy hillsides, especially where bordering woodland offers safe retreat.

The woodchuck is one of the great sleepers of the mammal world. He passes the time of cold and sleet and snow comfortably snuggled at the

New York Zoological Society

end of his burrow deep under ground in a state of almost suspended animation. He feeds on grasses, clover, and various cultivated crops, especially vegetables, but, unlike many rodents, he does not lay up stores of food for the winter. As summer draws to an end, he feeds heavily and waxes excessively fat. At the approach of cold weather he becomes more and more sluggish, and in late October, or early November, he retires to his burrow and begins the hibernating sleep. During this time, his heart beats only fourteen times a minute instead of almost a hundred, and in ten minutes he will have but a single respiration followed by ten or fifteen breaths. Normally he would breathe eighty or ninety times a minute.

On "Ground Hog Day," February second, he is supposed to wake from his long winter's sleep to look about and survey the weather. If the sun shines so that he can see his shadow, bad weather is indicated and he retires to resume his sleep for another six weeks. Otherwise the winter is broken and mild weather is predicted. Many country men still appraise the character of coming spring by the weather on Ground Hog Day. It is hardly necessary to say that this is largely a matter of superstition, although sometimes, between February and April, in the warmer parts of their range, woodchucks do come forth to resume their seasonal activities.

The Sea Cow's Ballast Tanks

IF you want to keep your fairy tale belief that a mermaid is a beautiful maiden with blond flowing hair, don't look at the creature which forms the basis for the legend. The real mermaid is a fat brunet animal, physically unattractive, named the dugong.

When the Arab traders, cruising down the Red Sea or on their way to Madagascar, caught a glimpse of the round head of a dugong peering above the waves, or saw a mother with a baby tucked under her arm, they naturally thought of it as being in some way human. A seal does not look much like a man, yet anyone who has seen a seal's head bobbing above the waves will know how much it resembles a human being. Given such a start, together with the fact that the dugong has a broad forked tail, a little imagination could easily populate the mysterious depths of the ocean with a strange folk, half human, half fish.

Another claim to distinction is that the hide of the dugong is believed to have been used by the Israelites to cover the Ark of the Covenant. This legend is indicated in its scientific name, *Helicore tabernaculi*.

One of the largest members of the sea cow family, *Rhytina*, which lived in the Bering Sea, was exterminated—literally "eaten off the face of the earth" —by sea otter hunters who discovered that the flesh of the animals was like excellent beef. The living family is widely distributed. One lives in the rivers of West Africa, another in parts of Florida, a third in the Red Sea, and a near relative on the coast of Australia.

The bones of all sea cows are extremely dense and heavy, being almost ivorylike in texture. This weight of bone is believed to serve the same purpose as the ballast tanks of a submarine; it helps to keep the animal submerged so that it can browse on aquatic plants.

From a drawing by Nino Carbe

This Okapi Stayed Home

HALF a century ago a piece of striped animal skin from the Congo region of Africa was brought by natives to the famous explorer, Sir Harry Johnston. He sent it to the British Museum, and it was thought to be a new species of zebra. Later, when a skin and two skulls reached London, it was discovered that the okapi, as the natives called it, had no relationship to the zebra. Actually it is a giraffe and a veritable "living fossil" akin to the extinct *Palaestragus*. For fifteen million years or more, it has been quietly plodding up the hill of time, changing almost not at all.

Why did the okapi not become extinct millions of years ago? No one knows. Today, it is one of the rarest and shyest of all large mammals, living deep in the gloomy forests of the Belgian Congo. Perhaps that is the reason why it has held over from the Miocene Period. While other giraffes with more ambition were developing long legs and elongated necks and living out on the open plains, the okapi kept to the quiet darkness of the tropical forests where the struggle for existence was not so great. Be that as it may, the fact remains that all his relatives, except the big spotted fellow, lived their alloted span and died while it went on.

Walking Stick

MIMICRY as a protective device of nature may be either active or passive. The chameleon is an example of active mimicry—it changes its color constantly to resemble its background.

The best known of all cases of passive mimicry are those astonishing insects called the walking sticks (*Aplopus mayeri*), which look so much like sticks, or stems, that one has difficulty in distinguishing all their parts from the twigs among which they live. You'll find the walking stick almost anywhere in America where there are twigs, but you'll have to look very close.

His Snout is a Sword

THE scientific name of the swordfish is *Xiphias gladius*, meaning sword in both Greek and Latin. His shape is somewhat like that of a mackerel, and from tail to snout he is built on racing lines. He is the personification of symmetry, beauty, and grace. Nevertheless, his huge staring eyes and his upper jaw and snout, which are prolonged into a horizontally flattened, dagger-edged sword, give him a formidable appearance. His record weight is close to nine hundred pounds. He uses the sword to kill other fish for his food.

On calm days *Xiphias* loves to loaf at the surface and bask in the sunlight. Thus he can be seen from the masthead of a vessel at a distance of two or three miles. Strangely enough a basking swordfish possesses little fear of a plunging schooner but does seem to dread a small boat.

Many authenticated reports of swordfish attacking boats are known in scientific literature. Off Block Island, New York, Captain Alfred Cyr narrowly escaped serious injury when a fish charged the small boat he was in, ran its sword through the craft, and wounded him in the chest. Near Montauk, Long Island, Mr. John Maxson of the schooner *Adelaide T.*, harpooned a big swordfish from his vessel and had gone out in a dory to finish it off with a lance. He hauled on the line until the fish was about ten feet away. Then, without warning, it turned furiously and drove its sword full length into the dory's side at the waterline. Why do swordfish attack boats? Apparently it is usually done when the killing lance strikes the fish in the head or in the spinal column near the head. Then the fish seems to go crazy and dashes madly at the nearest object.

Swordfishing is an ancient business. As far back as the year 100 B.C. it was carried on in the Strait of Messina as it is today.

He Combines Features of Each

THE duckbill, or platypus, *Ornithohynchus anatinus*, is a mammal but he has some very important non-mammalian features. He's at home on land as well as in water. He has the wide flat bill and the webbed feet of a duck and is an excellent swimmer, but though his feet are flat and his legs are short he can run very fast on land and his home is a burrow on the bank of a stream or pond. The female platypus lays eggs as birds do but nurses its young as mammals do. When the eggs hatch, the mother duckbill makes a sort of pouch for her hairless babies by folding back her tail underneath her and she keeps her young there until they have grown their fur.

The platypus eats land food such as worms, snails and insects, and it has cheek pouches in which it pockets the food it gathers. In effect, the platypus has adapted from many sorts of animals the features that are best for himself.

[183]

Undersea Seduction

UNLIKE the wild flower which it resembles in name and rivals in beauty, the sea anemone is neither a plant nor a harmless decoration.

It belongs to the animal kingdom and preys upon small sea animals, which are attracted to its petal-like, poison-laden tentacles. So alluring are some anemones and so quickly acting their poisons that certain species of crabs use the anemones to catch and kill marine animals for food.

Shock-Absorber Spikes

THE sea urchin (*Strongylocentrotus drobachiensis*) is one of the most perfectly protected creatures of the submarine world.

Completely covered with long, sharp spines, it presents a forbidding surface to attackers. The spines also act as shock absorbers against the force of the waves and sudden violent contact with the rocks. The sea urchin need make no effort to defend itself, for its natural armor is protection enough.

Animal Allies

THROUGHOUT nature there are any number of examples of dissimilar creatures living together not only in harmony but also on a mutual-aid co-operative basis. This sort of animal partnership is called symbiosis. Everyone knows the fable of the lion and the mouse but symbiosis, the way certain creatures complement each other and exist to mutual advantage, goes far beyond this example.

A striking instance of this mutual benefit type of animal society is the case of the clown fish and the sea anemone. The sea anemone, shown and described elsewhere in these pages, is a rather fearsome thing. Its tentacles contain poisonous stinging cells, but they never bother the clown fish, which is a damselfish called *Amphiprion percula*. The clown fish lives in such close association with the sea anemone that it is sometimes called the sea anemone fish. Its home is among the tentacles of the sea anemone, a safe place, for the clown fish's enemies will stay away from the poisonous sea anemone and the sea anemone itself will not bother its associate. If not for this refuge the clown fish would probably be extinct because it is a slow swimmer and its bright colors are highly conspicuous. Another contribution by the anemone to the clown fish is the food supply it provides for the young clown fish which feed on bits from the anemone's haul.

But what does the clown fish do for the anemone? One thing we know is that the sea anemone does thrive better when there are clown fish around. In some cases the clown fish does go out and bring tasty bits of food to the anemone. It has been reported also that the clown fish appears to provide a sort of "massage" and a sort of "air-conditioning" service to the anemone. It rubs up against it and fans it and that seems to improve the animal's health, particularly when the condition of the sea water becomes unfavorable for one reason or another.

Whether the contributions of the partners are disproportionate or not, here nature shows the co-operative way to survival.

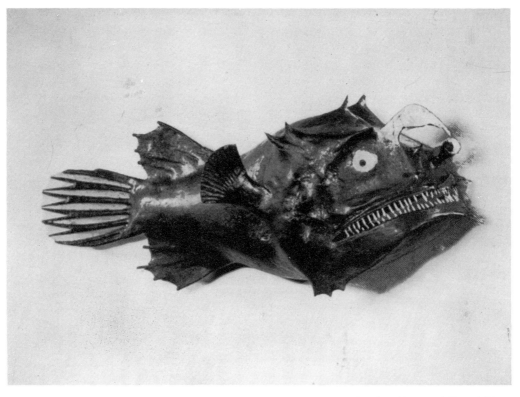

Her Husband Is Permanently Attached To Her

CERTAIN little fish of the Ceratidae family known as black seadevils which dwell deep in the sea have a unique family arrangement. The female carries her husband permanently attached to her head, and the wife is the sole supporter of this family. Many times the size of her mate, she has a huge mouth with sharp spiny teeth. The wife not only supplies transportation to her husband, but also his food.

The male is attached to the female by his mouth and soon after the larval stage, he grafts himself onto her body. The outer skin of the two is continuous and the blood systems are blended. Thus the male is fed without either having to hunt or even eat his food.

This black seadevil which inhabits the perpetually dark depths of the ocean carries around on the end of her nose a phosphorescent headlight to blind and lure her prey into her cavernous mouth.

It was first discovered in the Gulf of Panama and apparently is quite rare. This may be due to the fact that few males can find females in the abysmal darkness. It is probably only by accident that they meet, but nature has provided a way for them to stick together once they meet.

The male, at first glance, looks like a mere appendage swinging from the head of the female but it really is a fish breathing through its own gills. In some cases more than one male attaches itself to one female and she supports several husbands.

The Obstetrical Toad

IN central and southwestern Europe there is a frog who has a good claim to the Cautionary Championship of the animal world. To be absolutely sure his eggs will not be destroyed, to give his young their best chance to grow to maturity, he attaches the eggs to himself and keeps them with him all the time until they are hatched.

The obstetrical toad, *Alytes obstetricans,* does not risk the hazards of nests or pools. Instead, when the eggs are laid by the female, he ties them around his hind legs and carries this nursery about with him, giving his young a month of development before he releases them to face the world. The eggs come out tied together by a cord a yard or more long, and it is a simple matter for the toad to take up his brood and perform his parental function.

Huff and Puff

THE puffer has a simple way of protecting itself—it blows itself up when threatened, disturbed or in a huff. An eight-inch fish can swallow a quart of water during its puffing act or it can puff itself up with air and float, belly up, to the surface. When puffers inflate they become hard as footballs. At a very early age, when they are only one-quarter of an inch long, young puffers begin to show some of their puffing tricks. Their

bodies are extremely distensible and they look like peas.

There are many species of puffers which are called also globefish, swell-fish and are of the order *Plectoganthi*. Probably the most spectacular of the puffers is the porcupine fish which is armored with sharp and extremely disagreeable spines. It does not inflate itself quite so much as other puffers. (It is commonly sold in preserved condition, as a curiosity.) Harper's Swellfish, also shown, is more like the typical puffer. Puffers are found rather generally in the warmer parts of the Atlantic and Pacific.

New York Zoological Society

The Gnu's Front Bumper

GNUS are sometimes called "horned horses." They have horselike bodies and both sexes have horns which curve downward and outward, then up, serving, particularly in older animals, as front bumpers or even as helmets. The horns are stout, sharply pointed and dangerous. Gnus, members of the genus *Connochetes* of the antelope family, are sometimes called wildebeests. The most common species is the white-bearded gnu which inhabits South and East Africa. A related species, the white-tailed gnu or black wildebeest which formerly was abundant in South Africa, is almost extinct now. It could not find refuge in the desert, as many other animals did, simply because it had to have water and it did not develop a self-contained water supply as certain other animals did.

[191]

The "Fish" That Uses Fishing Tackle

THE Portuguese man-of-war, *Physalia*, lives in the deep blue waters of all warm seas. It is not a jellyfish, as is commonly believed, but is a coelenterate like the sea anemone. *Physalia* lives on top of the water and looks like a beautiful bluish float. But he has long, translucent, streamer-like tentacles that droop into the water. All along the streamers are tiny pear-shaped nettles, or stinging hairs, containing a killing springlike thread. As the tentacle comes into contact with another creature, a trigger-shaped mechanism automatically releases the thread with its springlike point which, carrying a substance similar to the acid found in bees, shoots out. This "sting" is effective enough to puncture human skin, the victim suffering spasm, shock, and several days prostration. It is as if he were stung by a swarm of bees.

Of course, for any kind of little fish (save one, *Nomeus*) a Portuguese man-of-war is deadly. The fish is suddenly stung and paralyzed; then the *Physalia's* tentacles pull the hapless fish up to its little sucking mouths which spread, funnel-like, over it to start the process of ingestion. Why the bluish fish, *Nomeus*, is safe and protected by the Portuguese man-of-war is a mystery. It provides them with food as well as shelter, for, like dogs enjoying scraps from the table, they feed upon the particles of food discarded by *Physalia*. It may be that *Nomeus* serves as a lure. Other fishes, seeing them swimming about in the danger zone, venture in, nibble on a tentacle, and provide food for both *Physalia* and *Nomeus*.

A Lizard that's Strong Enough to Kill a Horse

THE most terrible dinosaur that ever breathed was *Tyrannosaurus rex*, the king of tyrants. He lived a hundred million years ago and left no modern relative behind him.

Still there is a lizard which exists today on the island of Komodo in the Dutch East Indies that might be his first cousin so far as superficial resemblance is concerned. Moreover, it is the biggest lizard on earth and is just about king of his island world. The lizard's scientific name is *Varanus komodensis*, and he is big enough and strong enough to kill a horse. Actually he doesn't grow more than ten feet in length, or weigh more than two hundred and fifty pounds, but that is a pretty big lizard.

When Mr. Douglas Burden watched one of these giants lumbering down a hillside through the tropical jungle, he said it seemed like a *Tyrannosaurus rex* come to life. The impression was more vivid, too, as the creature leaped upon the carcass of a pig and buried its jaws in the meat. Seesawing back and forth, legs braced, it tore out great chunks of flesh with its enormous teeth, swallowing them at a gulp. One big fellow took in the whole hind quarter of a deer—hooves, legs, hams, and vertebrae—crowded it into his mouth and down his throat. *Tyrannosaurus* must have acted that way, only his prey was other dinosaurs.

The animals of Komodo Island flee in terror from the big lizards just as

other dinosaurs made way for the king of tyrants a hundred million years ago.

There is a marked resemblance between *Varanus komodensis* and the Chuckwalla lizard, but *Varanus* is much larger and heavier.

The Flowers' Revenge

THERE is a group of plants, called insectivorous, that reverses the usual relationship of insects and flowers. As a rule, bees, butter-flies and other such insects feed on plants but the pitcher plant, *Sarracenia purpurea,* from New England, turns the tables and eats whatever insects it can trap into its wide enveloping petals. There are many varieties of pitcher plants. Some contain water in which the insects dissolve, others digest the insects with the aid of acid secretions.

The Venus's-flytrap, from the Carolinas, is another insect-eating plant and there are many others all over the world.

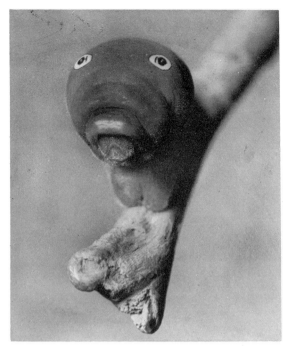

Insect Cinderella

OU see on this page one of the ugliest caterpillars in existence. It is grotesque to the point of being repulsive. Those fierce eyes, green and yellow with black and blue pupils, rather like the painted eyes of a clown, look unreal. And the answer is that they are not eyes at all, but eye-spots. The true eyes are located further down on the head. Located in front

of the eye-spots are openings for two fleshy "horns" which give off a nauseating odor when they are thrust forth. When an enemy comes near, this caterpillar rocks itself back and forth, presenting altogether a rather disagreeable, fearsome and dangerous front—the fierce look, the horrible smell and the fighting movement.

It passes through the winter in this ugliness, which helps it to survive, and then it emerges into one of the most beautiful of butterflies—Tiger Swallowtail, *Papilio glaucus.*

Black Star

INDEX

INDEX